HIDDEN HISTORY
of CIVIL WAR
TENNESSEE

State capital of Nashville during the Civil War. *Hoobler Collection, Tennessee State Library and Archives.*

HIDDEN HISTORY
of CIVIL WAR
TENNESSEE

JAMES B. JONES JR.

THE
History
PRESS

Published by The History Press
Charleston, SC 29403
www.historypress.net

First published 2013

Manufactured in the United States

ISBN 978.1.60949.899.3

Library of Congress Cataloging-in-Publication Data

Jones, James B., 1947-
Hidden history of Civil War Tennessee / James B. Jones Jr.
p. cm. -- (Hidden history)
ISBN 978-1-60949-899-3 (pbk.)
1. Tennessee--History--Civil War, 1861-1865. 2. United States--History--Civil War, 1861-
1865. I. Title.
E579.J66 2013
976.8'04--dc23
2013024338

CONTENTS

TENNESSEE IN THE CIVIL WAR

More than Before

A bout fifteen years ago, I asked a colleague how many military engagements took place in Tennessee during the Civil War. He immediately piped up with the established answer provided by E.B. Long in his book *The Civil War*, that there were 1,462 fights in the Volunteer State during the Civil War[1]—"second only to Virginia," my friend said, in genuinely reverential tones. I thought my search had ended before it began, but I took a look at Long's work only to find that he did not indicate how he got his sum.

Using Long's figure of 1,462 cases of belligerency in Tennessee from 1861 to 1865, an interesting estimate can be made that raises questions about the actual amount of time spent in combat.[2] After taking into account the length of battles such as Fort Donelson, Shiloh, Stones River, Chattanooga, Knoxville and Nashville (two weeks each), I assigned the arbitrary but rational value of three hours to all military conflicts in the state; the total number of hours spent in combat was thus 4,386 hours (or 183 days). The total number of hours Tennessee was involved in the war amounts to 35,874 (or 1,491 days). Thus, the time spent in actual fighting was 12 percent of the total. Didn't anything else transpire during the other 88 percent (1,308 days) of the time? Even after tripling the value of *all* combat to an average of 9 hours, only 36 percent of the time was spent in actual fighting. It was impossible to make a comparison because no such similar conjecture had been made. Nevertheless, by these calculations, the actual time spent in combat in Tennessee during the Civil War appears to have been less than half. Thus, even Nathan Bedford Forrest, the inexhaustible and famous Confederate cavalry hero, could rest and reload sometimes.

These calculations spurred my interest, and so I consulted Frederick H. Dyer's *Compendium* for numbers and documentation. At first, I was delighted at this book of lists, but I soon found that Dyer offered no sources, only the briefest of descriptions that accounted only for Federal units. Since no Confederate units were named, I imagined that the Union forces fought phantoms. A more detailed study led to the "Guide Index" of the National Park Service study entitled *Military Operations of the Civil War*. This promising publication indicated the kind of military action that occurred at the given time and place. This was encouraging, but it provided a minimum of narrative value, did not go much beyond the listing of military events and did not place them in chronological order.[3]

I hadn't found what I was looking for: a chronological, documented list of martial conflicts in Tennessee that provided narration based on the *Official Records (OR)*.[4] Either I was to drop the project or do the right thing: take it upon myself to do the work of the historian, to seek out new information and to boldly go where many had gone before—to the *OR*. At first, I intended to come up with a more accurate list of combat and dates preceding the operational reports found within the *OR*, but these were not keyed to report citations. However, by pasting them together, I saw a limited chronology begin to emerge.

So, there was nothing else to do but count them. I reasoned that the only place to find the information was in the *OR*'s two-volume index. It was a matter of counting beans. I went page by page, entry by entry, seven times in all, and finally concluded that there was something over 1,700 separate instances of combat, most of them accompanied by at least one circumstantial report. This list was matched to Dyer's list, which proved to be manifestly lacking by comparison. My documented list was bigger, and so I concluded that I had found the documentation with which I could construct the narrated list for which I was hunting.

This meant keying in what seemed an endless number of reports on skirmishes, reconnaissance, bushwhacking, conscript sweeps, naval combat and other lesser events that were separate and distinct actions not mentioned in circumstantial combat reports or the index. These citations would have been next to impossible to enumerate without the aid of the CD-ROM technology.[5]

I found that the *Official Army and Navy* records provided excellent and credible accounts, but I still wanted independent corroboration. What better sources than newspapers, diaries and correspondence? These familiar sources did not provide many beans for the combat incidents counter's mill. They did, though, address the gloomy psychological aspects of the war on the homefront, politics, displacement and the plight of refugees, confiscation of property, guerrilla warfare, smuggling, inflation, currency and commodities speculation, food shortages, urban life, myriad Special and General Orders not recorded in the *OR*, attempts to improve public health, public education, the complexity of occupation, the roles played by women, religious and family life, murders, politics, the theater, juvenile delinquency, prostitution, murder, the liberation and shaping of the African American community and the effect of the war on children, to name but a few. There was more to the war in Tennessee than, as my neighbor's nine-year-old son put it, "neat fightin' stuff."

Tabulations so far indicate 2,777 instances of combat in Civil War Tennessee. Until now, Virginia was held to be the state where most Civil War combat took place. The Old Dominion's total, according to Long, was 2,154—623 less than the newly tabulated total for Tennessee. So, if nothing else, one may conclude that there was more fighting in the Volunteer State than in any other state. That being the case, it is possible to suggest that the war was won (or lost) in Tennessee, not Virginia. For those who may censure this finding with discriminating remarks with reference to "quality versus quantity," I say that quantity has a quality all its own. Virginia might regain its earlier ascendant place as the "mother of all Civil War battles" when someone does as I did and heeds Casey Stengel's admonishment: "You can look it up." It has been transferred to an online site for easier access to the public.[6]

The nature of the fighting in Tennessee was not characterized by large battles. Instead, combat was mostly on the smaller level of the skirmish, at 1,122, or roughly 40 percent of the total. The other 60 percent of combat missions is divided between "affairs," reconnaissance, raids, guerrilla action and what we might today call "search and destroy" missions, expeditions of various types and, of course, battles.

The terminology for the various kinds of combat activity defied any settled definitions. They knew what they meant when they meant it.[7] Could a "skirmish" be identified by numbers of combatants? No, as a skirmish could involve as few as seven with no losses or as many as seven thousand men with losses amounting to eighty.[8] A skirmish could precede a large battle or be an isolated incident. An "action" could not be determined to be any different from an "engagement," and at times, a "scout" meant reconnaissance, and vice versa. The Tennessee total of 2,777 incidences cannot represent an all-inclusive number of combat operations in Tennessee during the Civil

War. For example, my findings show fifty-eight citations under the word "skirmishes." How many were "skirmishes"? Three? Fifteen? Similarly, how is an "affair" different from an "engagement" or a "retreat" from a "withdrawal"? There was no designation "conscript sweep" in any of the *OR* circumstantial combat reports or indexes. Many references to conscripting activity are found serendipitously in correspondence, newspaper reports and journals. I have found nothing to indicate how conscripting actually worked. One hint comes from Brigadier General Gideon J. Pillow in January 1863. As conscription officer for the Army of Tennessee, he reported to General Braxton Bragg that he had ordered his field commanders

> *to rake Bedford County, in which there are 1,500 men liable to duty under the conscript law. I was anxious to clean out that county by one movement, and doing it at once to avoid giving alarm.*
>
> *A partial movement over one portion of the county will give the alarm, and cause the conscripts to scatter and hide out.*[9]

So, not only was there some reluctance to join the Confederate army, but being conscripted was also more accurately a swift, jolting experience, with cavalrymen dragooning farm boys against their will. Why else would Pillow fear that they would scatter and hide out? Scattering and hiding out were contradictory to my own accepted notions of Confederate youth eager to follow the Rebel battle flag. Likewise was the apparent opposition to enlisting in the Confederate army by some young men in the cities.[10]

Among the insights I found startling was the general calm and resignation displayed in newspapers concerning the February 1861 vote to stay in the Union. The secret nature of the business of the legislature was equally curious, especially after the awe-inspiring pro-Union vote in February. Why was it secret? What went on behind closed doors? Another insight revolved around the attempt of the state government to finance its war effort. It was pitiful, even comical. Men of means and position agitated more about the transfer of state debt to the Confederate government and having it reimburse bondholders for expenses than they did about providing for soldiers' needs. In late January 1862, it was obvious to the members of the Fayetteville Committee of Correspondence that volunteers from Lincoln County would get no winter clothing from the Confederate government. They wrote a truly touching letter to Confederate secretary of war L.P. Walker, offering to clothe them with uniforms made from wool textiles manufactured in Fayetteville. Flush with promises of huge profits, arms manufacturers promised state officials the moon but could not deliver, forcing the governor to impound all civilian sporting pieces for military use.

The formation of refugee juvenile gangs in the cities in 1864 also came as a surprise. One gang, called the "Forty Thieves," originated in Louisville and spread down the railroad to Nashville, Chattanooga and even Atlanta. Another, the "Mackerel Brigade," formed in Memphis. Turf battles were fought with rival gangs that came from New Orleans. The magnitude of illegal cotton trading near Memphis, Chattanooga and in middle Tennessee was also intriguing. The editor of the *Chattanooga Daily Rebel* was infuriated about it, as was Major General William Tecumseh Sherman in Memphis. The War Department quietly sanctioned the practice.

Inflated prices and currency and commodities speculation were common, but the anti-Semitism displayed by Grant and Sherman was previously unknown to me. I know some may find this an onerous conclusion, but Nathan Bedford Forrest was defeated a number of times in Tennessee. There was at least one case of mass murder of United States Colored Troops' officers and soldiers committed by Confederate soldiers under Forrest's command. The incidence and extent of guerrilla (or, as some prefer, "partisan ranger") activity and the extreme measures taken to suppress it were widespread. Home guard units on both sides often took on characteristics of terrorist gangs and were only in it for the money. Colonel Fielding Hurst (U.S.), for example, extorted more than $100,000 from citizens of west Tennessee, while his brother-in-law squeezed $50,000 out of McNairy County alone. Both Confederate and Federal forces took political prisoners and hostages to extort loyalty. Evidence was found regarding the vigilante-like behavior of the numerous "Committees of Public Safety" that formed in Memphis and Nashville before fighting took place. Such groups were apparently as much mechanisms for slave and class management as instruments to appropriate the wealth of those whose beliefs were not "pc" ("politically Confederate").

Another unique chapter of the war in Tennessee cities dealt with the U.S. Army Medical Corps and prostitution. The practice was unquestionably a great threat to the army, and in 1863, officials in Nashville exiled the courtesans to Louisville. The "Cyprians" weren't welcomed there and were restored to Nashville. The only solution was to set up a legalized and licensed system of prostitution based on medical inspection. Memphis duplicated the system a year later. Additionally, the medical corps made strides in improving and maintaining public health, constructing sewers; removing dead animals, rubbish and offal from the streets; and enforcing smallpox inoculation. Early in the war, the Southern Mothers formed in Memphis, as well as similar groups in other cities, to help sustain and nurse wounded Confederate troops. However, as wounds festered, the well-mannered belles of Memphis were reluctant to continue in their roles as caregivers. Sixty-four bellicose belles of Gordonsville, Smith County, petitioned Governor Johnson in November 1862 for arms, which they wished to use in "aiding to put down the rebellion." "If you accept us," they wrote, "please send them immediately...If not we will arm ourselves and bushwhack it." They were not at all like the pro-Confederate and wealthy Rebecca Carter Craighead of Nashville, who refused to take the oath of allegiance to the Union until she wanted to take a trip to New York City in the summer of 1864.[11] She quickly swore the oath and took her trip, where she purchased a $400 dress and fine jewelry.[12] One east Tennessee woman, angry that her husband had joined the Confederate army, declared, "Cust [sic] if ever he sleeps in my bed again."[13]

There was poetry in the newspapers, as well as accounts of flag or sword presentations, humorous accounts of grand balls and camp life and editorials complaining of martial prohibition. The theater was active in the cities. In February 1864, John Wilkes Booth appeared in Nashville and got rave reviews.[14] An interesting comment on class consciousness is found in a letter from Lieutenant General Leonidas Polk to his wife, written in February 1863. He mentioned that he promoted his son to his staff because the young man found the artillery captain to whom he was assigned too demanding. While Confederate soldiers went without, Polk sent his wife material and dress patterns. He complained that his staff officers were too busy seeking paramours about the countryside to write their reports on the Battle of Stones River.[15]

In the months before the fiasco at Fort Donelson, slave owners were asked to provide labor to help build fortifications at Nashville and other points. Few did, and some bragged about not complying. The forts weren't built. It struck me as ironic that the very people who had the most to gain from the Confederacy refused to support it, and not out of loyalty to the Union but out of a stingy spirit of deception and duping the government. In middle Tennessee, at least, a sort of sliding scale of class consciousness and prejudice existed in which the poorest whites resented the Confederacy for conscripting their sons to fight a rich man's war. The middle class, while supportive of the Confederacy, was ambivalent. The richest were the most stalwart in their support of the rebellion and often sent Confederate foraging parties to those they considered traitors to the cause.

Other insights included the October 1863 proposal by Nashvillian S.R. Cockrill to the Commissioners of the Confederate States for a five-step strategy to harvest fish in Tennessee's rivers to feed the armies. General Pillow endorsed the idea and proposed using his conscription force to aid in the plan. In February 1865, the State of Tennessee Board of Commissioners met in Aberdeen, Mississippi. The men worked long and hard to establish an extensive "schedule of prices for produce and army supplies…to continue in force until altered." That there was no Confederate authority in Tennessee that late in the war apparently did not cross their minds. General Pillow, by the way, on two separate occasions wrote to the Federal commanders in Memphis in attempts to obtain safe passage so that he might take care of his property within Union lines. If this wasn't treasonous (as well as stupid), it was very close.

Another insight into the war was finding the location of the first recorded instance of actual fighting in Tennessee—it had to start somewhere. The site was on the Cumberland Plateau, near the Kentucky border, in Pickett County at a place called Travisville. This was a new finding to historians and the natives. In time, a historical marker was unveiled to an appreciative crowd of locals and politicians. A forty-page booklet entitled *A Documentary Guide to the Civil War on the Tennessee Cumberland Plateau* was produced, and given its limited run of 120 copies, it was out of print in a week. This was an insight that led me to entrepreneurial musings about profiting from history and new notions about history education—namely, documentary evidence was a popular commodity and a teaching tool.

This reference book approach to the Civil War in Tennessee can have a more populist application. I like to think that as a printed text, this work will prove of interest to "civilians" who have neither the time nor the research skills to find this data. The public has no familiarity with such documents because of a number of factors, the most compelling being that it is difficult to find where they are located in primary sources, especially the *OR*. It simply bewilders them. This brings up the point of the professional versus avocational expenditure of the time it takes to conduct research. In west Tennessee's Civil War history, there was a skirmish on June 30, 1862, at a place then called both Morning Sun or Rising Sun—a Confederate victory, by the way. One constituent, an elderly enthusiast, said that he had spent most of his adult life looking for any information about the fight but could not find it. He didn't know where to look. I knew where to look and provided him with that information within minutes. It wasn't that hard to do, but then I'm a historian. He could have "cut to the chase" had there been a documentary guide to the Civil War in Tennessee for him to consult.

While this compilation cannot be called comprehensive, it is big. It presents more diversity that can help refocus attention away from a nearly unilateral fixation with "neat fightin' stuff" to a better understanding of the complexity of the war in Tennessee. It can serve an educational function and maybe even attenuate the dogged "us versus them" thinking, what one writer identifies as a "neo-Confederate mentality." That approach interprets the war as a uniformly martial white male Southern heritage, the product of the United Daughters of the Confederacy's successful efforts that "distorted why the South seceded and made hash of Civil War history from beginning to end."[16] We need to be wary of the "heritage syndrome," or an inclination to remember what is charismatic or pleasing and to discount the rest.[17] History and heritage, it follows, are two different things. It might be best to reflect on the phrase, "We weren't there; we didn't do that." The counterfactual way of interpretation ("what if") should be avoided. History is, by definition, irrevocable.

This book presents essays, based on solid documentation, to assist the reader to reach an understanding that there is more to the Civil War than before. The essays point out hidden chapters in Tennessee's Civil War experience[18] that were unknown because of former emphasis on famous generals and "their" battles. It is envisioned to give the reader the view that, as Harry S Truman once said, "the only thing new is the history you don't know."

AUTHOR'S NOTE

Information in this book was gleaned from articles in the *Tennessee Historical Quarterly*; the *West Tennessee Historical Society Papers*; the *Courier*, the newsletter of the Tennessee Historical Commission; *North & South Magazine*; *Civil War History*; and other original presentations of formerly unpublished work by the author.

Chapter 1

A HISTORY OF COMMITTEES OF SAFETY AND VIGILANCE IN WEST AND MIDDLE TENNESSEE, 1860–1862

C ivil War Committees of Vigilance (or Safety) evolved from antecedents in the antebellum South. In the more immediate sense, they derived from the Minute Man organizations, John C. Breckenridge's "political clubs" in the election of 1860.[19] For example, a report in Memphis on December 12, 1860, presents a direct connection between the Minute Men and a Vigilance Committee (also called, interchangeably, Committee of Vigilance) when the pilot of a steamboat was discovered "tampering with a negro." "The Vigilance Committee of the Minute Men arrested him, and, after a trial, he was told to leave town instanter." The same day, the Minute Men were searching the city for an abolitionist. Nailing him to a tree would be an apt punishment, noted the *Memphis Avalanche*.[20]

In Memphis, days after the bombardment of Fort Sumter, the Vigilance Committee was active. William Stevenson, a New Yorker on his way home from Texas, stopped for the night in Jeffersonville, Arkansas. His comments at dinner roused the suspicion of the local Vigilance Committee, whose members quizzed him but found nothing damning and Stevenson retired. They sent a midnight courier ahead, warning the Memphis Committee of Public Safety that a dangerous abolitionist would arrive later in the day.

No sooner had the New Yorker left the Memphis wharf when a "blue jacket," the paramilitary policemen guarding the city, greeted him, saying, "The Committee of Public Safety wish to see you, come along." He was lead to the committee, whose members inquired about his home, political opinions and destination. Then the committee introduced a member of the Jeffersonville Vigilance Committee who then testified as to the dangerous abolitionist character of the prisoner. But they were unable to find evidence of any crime, and the committee let him go.

He didn't get far. A blue jacket handed him a letter from the chairman suggesting that he enlist in the Provisional Army of Tennessee. It read, "Several members of the committee think if you do not see fit to follow this advice, you will probably stretch hemp." Stevenson wrote that "the military power in the city had resolved to *compel* me to *volunteer*...I wrote my name and thus I *volunteered*."[21]

The same day, the Committee of Public Safety in Memphis issued a proclamation. It announced that the committee had assumed sweeping powers, which the committee deemed necessary "being fully aware of its important and vital bearing upon the interests of its citizens." The committee now controlled access to all telegraph messages "that bear upon the peace and stability of the city...The military force of the city, as well as its municipal police, are all at their command...citizens...may rest assured... everything will be done...for their protection and safety."[22] The committee had effectively carried out a *coup de ville*.

It is uncertain when the Vigilance Committee formed. In Memphis, at least two other committee-like groups existed as well: the Memphis Board of Safety and the Memphis Military Committee.[23] There is less mystery about the creation of the Nashville Committee of Vigilance and Safety. Soon after the Confederate victory at Fort Sumter, a meeting was held at the capitol on April 24. Two resolutions were passed at the meeting: one, that Tennessee must join the Confederacy, and two, "Resolved, in...the position where in we suddenly find ourselves, the ordinary police regulations of this city seem to us utterly incompetent to exercise the vigilance imperative...in time of war...[therefore] we do earnestly recommend the immediate formation of a vigilance committee, invested with such enlarged powers as may give efficacy to their action, and constituted of some of our best known citizens acting in concert with the mayor and existing authorities."[24]

Something can be gleaned about the relative wealth and social standing of the names most prominently associated with the Memphis and Nashville Committees of Vigilance. Succinctly, they were men of wealth. The man most often mentioned as directing the Memphis committee's activities was Frazier Titus. The 1860 Federal Slave Census demonstrates that he owned twenty slaves, placing him in the top 10 percent of slave owners. Census data for Shelby and Davidson Counties[25] show that their vocations varied from "gentlemen" to railroad president, minister, plantation owner, contractors, banker and merchants. In Nashville, as stated in the resolutions of April 24, the Vigilance Committee was "constituted of…our best known citizens."

In Nashville, on the same day the Committee for Public Safety was forming, Mayor R.B. Cheatham issued his proclamation. All good citizens were requested to curb their enthusiasm and aid the authorities in preserving the peace of the city. According to his honor, "[S]elf-constituted Committees, or Individuals on their own responsibility, have notified one or more of our Northern-born Citizens to leave Nashville… This is…to notify all Persons that any complaints or suspicions against Persons of Northern birth can be lodged with me for investigation…all… will be protected [and]…properly investigated."[26]

The mayor's caution only stimulated activity leading to the formation of a Vigilance Committee. For example, a Cleveland, Ohio journeyman was expelled for expressing his Union sentiments after having been warned that such remarks were treasonable. He was deported by the nascent committee. Similar was the fate of editor of the *Nashville Democrat*, a Douglas paper. A mob threatened him and the destruction of his press. Determined to stand his ground, he barricaded the offices and raised the American flag. The mob was ready to lynch the editor and burn the newspaper office down. He was soon convinced to leave Nashville. The flag was lowered, and the committee occupied the office. No Northern man's life or property was safe in Nashville unless he declared himself a secessionist and blindly followed the Southern agenda.[27]

West and middle Tennessee, much less Nashville, were completely in the hands of the secessionists: "The…demagogues…constantly harangue the masses and the people seem to be insane on the subject of Southern rights…They…proclaim, that…one Southern man can whip a dozen Northern men." The evolution of a formal committee accelerated after the sudden rush to arms in the North following Lincoln's call for volunteers.[28] Davidson County's Committee of Vigilance and Safety was formed to protect the lives, property and interests of Nashville from the aggressive foe.[29] The *New York Times*, however, reported that "[i]n Nashville the Southern intolerants organized and put into operation a society which is miscalled 'The Committee of Safety.' It is the business of these men to spy out and denounce every man or woman suspected of Union proclivities, where upon follows an edict of banishment."[30]

Back in Memphis, the Vigilance Committee strongly suggested the efficacy of creating military units composed of free blacks. The idea was not a popular one among slave owners. Not content with such notions, the Vigilance Committee abolished worship services in black churches. Two weeks later, it softened its edict, so "that when the regular minister of a church, attended by *respectable white* persons, will agree to hold afternoon services, that the same be allowed."[31]

The Committee of Safety lived up to the *Times'* description. A day or two earlier, a young man left Memphis under rude circumstances. Upon leaving, he thoughtlessly remarked that if secessionists visited Fort Wayne, they would be clubbed. The cry of "abolitionist" was broached, and he was summarily knocked down, beaten and taken to a barber's shop, where his head was shaved. He was held overnight and sent north in the morning. Two weeks before this, a molder and two carpenters, thought to have returned north, "were seen hanging to trees a short distance from Memphis."[32]

The *Louisville Journal* spelled out the transformation that the Vigilance Committee had rendered: "Insane fury...posses their souls. They tolerate... tyranny...and...glory in upholding it...It is for the Committee to say who may live in the city...what newspapers...must be banned...what steamboat cargoes must be confiscated...who must be imprisoned, who whipped, who have his head shaved, who be tarred and feathered, and who hung."[33]

By late May, it was reckoned that the Vigilance Committee had driven out more than five thousand peaceable citizens and confiscated their property. This pogrom was stimulated by the February vote giving the pro-Union forces in the city a majority. Whether Southern- or Northern-born, the slightest suspicion of being an abolitionist caused the offender to be dragooned before the Committee of Safety and Frazier Titus, whose kangaroo court was constantly in session at Titus's block, processing an average of more than one hundred litigations a day. Cases ranged widely, including the conviction of a young Illinoisan charged with saying that he would not fight his friends in Cairo. He was ordered out of Memphis on the next northbound train. Eight men, after having their heads half shaved, were banished from Memphis, while three were under death sentences when they departed. One young Northern man who enlisted in the Rebel army for personal safety plaintively asked another Union man to help him escape. His plans were discovered by a "particularly obnoxious...party of secession ruffians" that left him little hope of leaving Memphis alive, even if he could not get a discharge.[34]

One widely printed account of a run-in with the Memphis Vigilance Committee by a Unionist-Tennessean told of his arrest, imprisonment and escape from the Bluff City. He was turned in to the committee by an erstwhile Northern man. In no city in Dixie "was there a larger population of Northern men who…had become…more Southern than the Southerner." They were "actuated…by the…desire to elevate themselves even to ignoble positions, if they promise[d] power and wealth."

He was suspected of writing a letter to the *New York Tribune* in March 1861[35] that expressed shock at the reception given to Mississippi soldiers on their way to Florida. The letter stimulated a visit by the Memphis Vigilance Committee, which examined his effects. The search gave him "a tickling sensation in the region of the thorax." After a complete inspection and many questions, he was "politely informed that they 'believed me to be a ___ Abolitionist,' and intended to settle my case in the morning." He was jailed, convinced that it was his last night on earth.

In the morning, he was ushered before the committee's court of sixty dour-faced men, all of whom wanted to execute him, and while there was no evidence to prove him a subversive, they decided to hold him until others could verify his opinions. He was thrown into a cell "equal to the famous 'Black hole of Calcutta.'" While there, he witnessed punishments meted out to the committee's victims. He saw more than eighty-five men have their heads shaved and as many whipped. He became inured to the daily floggings, but nothing prepared him for the sight of a Southern man "who would…lay the lash upon the back of an innocent and defenseless *woman*." On May 19, 1861, a young, beautiful, refined and accomplished lady from Maine, who had resided in Memphis for a year, was whipped for "expressing too loudly her wishes for the success of [Northern] arms." She had only the day before purchased steamer tickets, but she was arrested that evening and incarcerated for the night. At six o'clock the next morning, she was brought to the rear door of the jail, "and after *three* men had been whipped with the *knout*, and their heads shaved, *she was stripped to the waist, and thirteen lashes given her with a strap, and the right side of her head shaved.*"[36]

Such committees were not limited to larger cities such as Memphis. In the run-up to the June 8 vote on secession, the Brownsville Committee of Vigilance acted to slant the election's outcome. Reverend Cooper was head of the Female Seminary and a favorite in town. In May 1861, despite his popularity, a "delegation from the local committee of vigilance visited him and gave him his choice…to make a secession speech…enlist…or leave… town." He did neither, but a week later, he and other "abolitionists" received a preprinted and widely distributed[37] notice: "All citizens or residents among us of Northern or foreign birth will be allowed ten days to leave our community…but after that time [none]…shall be permitted to leave, but we shall expect all such to stand by…us…against invasion…by order of the Committee of Vigilance." Since no one could reasonably expect to dispose of property in ten days, the notice was an eviction and confiscation warning. Northerners and foreigners had but one realistic option: to leave without "stretching hemp." One witness from Tennessee testified that "he saw on the cars quite a number of men and women fleeing from other Tennessee towns." They "must, as they value their lives, vote for the disunion ordinance and devote themselves to the disunion cause."[38]

Meanwhile, back in Memphis, General P.G.T. Beauregard found himself the object of the committee's attention. He had "used great endeavors to keep his movements secret," but blue jackets jailed him as a spy. He was eventually identified and discharged.[39] The committee would make no mistakes on the secession referendum.

As the vote on secession approached, a veritable reign of terror developed in Tennessee. Notable was the exodus of Union sympathizers on the eve of the election. The *Louisville Journal* reported, "It would really seem as if when innumerable Vigilance Committees are daily and nightly at work throughout Tennessee expelling Union men and their families from the State [to stop them from voting]…on the 8th of June…they are afraid, that, notwithstanding the driving of thousands into exile and…turning…the… press…against the Union party, secession would still be voted down unless the polls should be girt with secession bayonets."[40]

The Tennessee Vigilance Committees had driven hundreds of those in opposition to the secession referendum out of the state without even the pretense of a legal trial and had taken it upon itself to search the mail for objectionable literature. Such activity was not sequestered to Memphis— middle Tennessee experienced the same. According to one report, "[T] he Vigilance Committee of Nashville usurps similar prerogatives… every day…the Vigilance Committees of Brownsville and other towns in Tennessee have given public notice to all men of Northern or foreign birth to leave the State…The Vigilance Committees…have ordained that each ballot cast shall be an open one…this will show who has the audacity to vote for the old Union—distinctly implying that whoever does so will do it at his deadly peril."[41]

As the vote approached, the Memphis Vigilance Committee distributed a broadside entitled *True Men of the South to the Rescue*. It was urgent that the secessionist vote be approved. The bulletin continued with anxious visions of enemies within, coupled with African American ruin, admonishing all business owners to "report immediately the names of all those who they know cannot be trusted." It was paramount this be done, otherwise "our gallant sons" in the field would live in dread that an enemy lurked at home to "incite our negroes to insurrection, and bring the worst calamities upon our wives, our mothers, and our daughters."[42]

Fiery rhetoric and assurances of doom were not enough to ensure victory. A more direct form of intimidation was resorted to on election day. Union men were marked on the day of the election by writing the name of each voter on the back of the ballot as it was entered on the poll book, with the corresponding number entered on both, so that after the election, Union ballots could easily be discovered and the voters attended to by the committee. This connivance was known prior to the election and successfully deterred Union men from voting or compelled them to vote for secession.[43] The story was the same in Yankeetown, the ironically named hamlet in White County, Tennessee. Some twenty Union men went to the polling station there and, seeing that their ballots were similarly marked, refused to vote. The thoughtful Amanda McDowell of the nearby Cherry Creek community recorded in her diary: "Frank Courtney voted Union…but things got so hot that he had to leave the grounds. And Jack said they marked him and were going after him last night… another man there swore that he did not think he would ever vote again, since it was of no use, that a man could not do as he wished like honest men ought to do, that their liberties had already been voted away by the 'big bugs' of the country…he did not know that he would ever vote again."[44]

These terrorist tactics, of course, produced a secessionist victory. And no wonder—nearly a month after the pro-secession vote, it was reported that more than six thousand people had "been driven from Memphis alone, by the edicts [of] the so-called Vigilance Committee, or through apprehension of mob violence." The exodus was similar in the middle and western sections of Tennessee.[45]

Charles Bolton's book *Poor Whites in the Antebellum South* argues that vigilance committees were particularly concerned with "guarding against…transient poor white men, who were perceived as…most susceptible to…appeals from the Republican Party."[46] This contention is illustrated by an incident that took place soon after the secessionist victory kindled and justified more attacks by Committees of Vigilance, especially in west Tennessee. Three young Kentuckians were hired out as deckhands on a coal barge to Natchez, Mississippi. Their work finished, they came back to Memphis expecting to continue to Louisville. However, the Memphis Vigilance Committee prohibited any boat from leaving for Louisville. The three couldn't afford train fare, so they were forced to walk.

At Covington, Tennessee, the three were arrested and examined by the Vigilance Committee. Nothing was found against them, and they were allowed to go on with a pass. They continued until rain stopped them about a mile from Ripley. They took refuge under a tree. Within minutes, mounted Tennesseans rode up and seized them as suspicious characters. They told their story and presented their pass. Nevertheless, some of the mounted men cursed them as abolitionists and demanded that they be hanged from the tree under which they were standing. The prisoners insisted that they were they were citizens of Kentucky and Louisville and that they were quiet workingmen with no sympathy for abolitionism. The fate of the three was doubtful, but at length, two were allowed to go. Because he gave a "short answer" to his interrogators, their other friend was executed. One of them recounted that between Memphis and Covington they came upon another victim of a Vigilance Committee, a beaten man lying "with his head shaved and his ears and the end of his nose cut off." This because he was of Northern birth.[17]

One incident revolving on the confiscation of a *Harper's Illustrated* sketch artist's luggage and its graphic rendering provides a face to the "Tennessee Taliban." The journal's artist was stopped in Memphis, where the Vigilance Committee rifled through his luggage. The members found a number of sketches and examined them carefully for anti-Southern nuances, "and each member…pocketed two or three of the most striking."[48]

Aside from the tame confiscation of an artist's sketches, hatred for Northerners remained robust. For example, one city justice in Memphis informed a Northern prisoner of his "profound regret that it was not in his power to hang him and…denounced him as a damned abolitionist…'Had I the power…I would cut your ears off, and nail you to the door of my court–room.'" This sort of terrorism was by now common, but punishment was not restricted to verbal abuse. The Memphis Vigilance Committee "went further…shaving the head and whipping being regarded as a slight punishment by anyone who desired to remove North…men were taken before the…Committee…and no one knows what became of them… Their acts are all secret…there is no concern for the men charged with… abolitionism, so that no one cares; and thus they go on in their wholesale murdering with impunity."[49]

Like his counterpart in Nashville, Memphis mayor John Park attempted to put a damper on the Vigilance Committee. A proclamation on August 24, 1861, indicated that the committee was pressing men into the service and committing violent acts outside the boundaries of civil law. According to Park, "Applications have repeatedly been made to me…for protection

Memphis Vigilance Committee inspecting a suspected spy's luggage. *From* Harper's Illustrated, *June 22, 1861.*

against…parties who…impress citizens into the service against their will… these men have been dragged from their beds, wives and children, but never has there been a man taken who had on a clean shirt.[50] I hereby notify any citizens who may wish to pass within the city of Memphis to call on me, and I will furnish the same,[51] and…he will be protected. One poor man being shot yesterday by one of these outlaws causes me to give [this] notice."[52]

One need only be traveling north to run afoul of a Vigilance Committee. In late August 1861, two parties arrived in Nashville from New Orleans. One of them bought tickets for his entire party, both men and women, and they boarded the car. But because they had no Vigilance Committee passports, they were herded off the train. All managed to find citizens to vouch for them, and passports were given. They left on the afternoon train and were surprised yet again at the Clarksville depot, when 140 personal letters and documents were taken from them to be carried back to the Nashville Vigilance Committee. Even a Confederate lieutenant returning from Richmond had 40 letters from his command to friends and family seized and taken to Nashville for scrutiny by the committee.[53]

The expulsion of Tennessee's Union citizens by Vigilance Committees was extended to one national figure. It was ironic and even more sensational when the self-constituted and extralegal Nashville Vigilance Committee summarily expelled United States Supreme Court associate justice John Catron.

Catron made a charge to a St. Louis grand jury, giving his views as to what constituted treason. His opinion created consternation in the Nashville Vigilance Committee. The *Nashville Gazette* observed that he had marked "thousands of...brave sons...[as] traitors, [that] he outrages the tenderest feelings of the fathers, mothers, brothers, sisters, wives and children of those gone to fight the battles of their country."[54] Yet the judge was not without friends. Stalwart secessionist V.K. Stevenson, president of the Nashville and Chattanooga Railroad, interviewed Catron in Nashville and was convinced that there was nothing dangerous in the judge's principles. He was certain that his presence in the capital would prove no threat to the Confederacy. Notwithstanding Stevenson's sincere endorsement, the Nashville Vigilance Committee delivered its ultimatum: either he would be forcibly driven out of his native Nashville or publicly support secession. He had twenty-four hours to decide. Catron chose to leave Nashville on an L&N train and arrived in Louisville.[55]

President Jefferson C. Davis's August 14, 1861 proclamation obliging all Northern men to leave within forty days made the local precedent national policy.[56] Two young printers from Philadelphia prepared to leave Nashville. The night before, they made a cordial visit on James T. Bell, the city editor of the *Daily Gazette*, to say goodbye. Bell told them that he could find no fault in their leaving. They shook hands and said adieu. Next morning, unknown to the two printers, an article appeared in Bell's department in the following morning's *Gazette* under the heading, "Stampede Among Printers." Bell portrayed them as a class of ingrates and spies. Ever since the Davis proclamation, printers "have been seen in groups upon our street corners...acting...as spies in our midst...Let us feel thankful that the proper means have been adopted to rid the cities of the South of such vampires." When the train stopped in Clarksville, the two were searched, harassed and threatened and had their belongings confiscated by the local Vigilance Committee.[57]

As the Federal armies occupied middle and west Tennessee, the Committees of Public Safety and Vigilance "skedaddled" from Nashville, Memphis and other venues. Little was said of them, although there was some taunting and satire. For example, soon after the mass departure of Confederate officials from Nashville, the *Louisville Journal* reported, "Nashville, if not taken, is evidently in peril. Where is her famous 'Vigilance Committee' that was so active a few months ago? Why doesn't it notify the United States army, as it did hundreds of private citizens, to leave within ten days?"[58] A satirical "review" of Reverend Dr. McFerrin's *Confederate Primer* pointed out that most merciful men were "the Nashville Vigilance Committee, for they saved their victims the suspense of a trial."[59]

Perhaps the most succinct comment on the nature of the Committees of Safety and Vigilance was a slogan seen on a banner in the grand procession commemorating the one-year anniversary of the fall of Memphis. It read simply: "The reign of terror of the Safety Committee has passed away forever."[60]

THE BATTLE AGAINST PROSTITUTION AND VENEREAL DISEASES IN CIVIL WAR NASHVILLE AND MEMPHIS

M ajor events and names in Tennessee's Civil War history are well known and well chronicled. Dramatic stories of big battles and exciting wartime biographies have dominated readers' attention. Until recently, however, very little attention has been paid to the medical and social aspects of Tennessee's Civil War experience. As one scholar recognized, "One contingency poorly prepared for...was medical care."[61] Both Nashville and Memphis became important centers for logistical, supply and medical activities during the conflict, and both cities were occupied by the United States Army. Where soldiers collected, it was nearly axiomatic that prostitutes would collect as well. Certainly the problem presented by prostitution and venereal disease was not planned for by the army, and it became a problem of major significance in Nashville and Memphis.

According to official medical records, "venereal diseases were associated with intemperance in the conditions which favored their causation." Incidence was higher "among troops stationed in the vicinity of cities among those on active service." Increases in the disease rate during the war corresponded with the additions of fresh levies of troops and the returns of furloughed veterans. In total, there were 73,382 cases of syphilis and 109,397 cases of gonorrhea reported among white soldiers in the Union army, resulting in 82 cases per 1,000 men. Among black troops, the corresponding figures were 34 cases per 1,000 for syphilis and 44 per 1,000 for gonorrhea. Thus, while not epidemic, venereal diseases were not unknown. The U.S. Army made efforts to limit the spread of these diseases among the troops, and the surgeon general reported that the "results were highly satisfactory."[62]

While specific protests concerning venereal diseases were not known to be extant, advertisements in Nashville newspapers for the period indicate that the problem was real. Dr. Coleman's Dispensary for Private Diseases, on North Cherry Street (now Fourth Avenue), catered to victims of venereal diseases. Dr. Richard A. Jones on Deaderick Street likewise offered treatments for "private diseases."[63]

In 1860, Nashville's red-light district was located "in quarter…two blocks wide and four blocks long, being the first block south of Spring [now Church] Street, on Front, Market, College, and Cherry (now First, Second, Third, and Fourth Avenues) Streets." The district, called Smokey Row, does not appear to have relocated elsewhere. In 1864, for example, a "house of ill fame" was located on College Street (now Third Avenue). Business was brisk, and the incidence of venereal disease skyrocketed. One private from Mahoning County, Ohio, Benton E. Dubbs, recalled that while he was in Nashville, "there was an old saying that no man could be a soldier unless he had gone through Smokey Row…The street was about three fourths of a mile long and every house or shanty on both sides was a house of ill fame. Women had no thought of dress or decency. They said Smokey Row killed more soldiers than the war."[64]

By June 1863, Brigadier General R.S. Granger, in command at Nashville, was "daily and almost hourly beset" by regimental commanders and surgeons seeking a means of ridding the city of the diseased prostitutes infesting it. Action was essential "to save the army from a fate worse…than to perish on the battlefield." Prostitution itself, though physically harmless, led to venereal disease and was equally "annoying and destructive to the morals of the army."[65]

Just after the Fourth of July, Provost Marshal Lieutenant Colonel George Spalding, Eighteenth Michigan Infantry, responded to pressure from superiors with a summary roundup and forced exile of all known prostitutes. The prostitutes' removal was a "military necessity." On July 6, the combined forces of the provost marshal and the city police force initiated the "removal of all women of ill-fame…which produced a considerable agitation in the northern part of the city." Spalding succeeded, and the "Cyprians" were put aboard the steamer *Idahoe* to be sent north. The exact number of women loaded onto the ship is not known; estimates ranged from 40 to 1,500 hundred.[66]

The operation was not gentle. "Squads of soldiers were engaged in… heaping furniture out of the various dens, and then tumbling their disconsolate owners after." The soldiers did not discriminate when making arrests, and so some "respectable ladies…were unceremoniously marched off." One newspaper hoped that "this course toward bad women will have a salutatory effect upon the morals of the soldiers."[67]

The women were sent to Louisville, Kentucky, on board the *Idahoe*, which was procured by the government "for the especial service of deporting the 'sinful fair.'"[68] The problem seemed well on its way to a final solution, but soon it became evident that extirpating all white prostitutes merely created a vacuum that was filled by black prostitutes. The rapid influx of contrabands into Nashville created a condition in which "a large number of the women [live] by prostitution…breeding disease which will spread like wild fire…So barefaced are these black prostitutes becoming [that] they parade the streets, and even public square, by day and night." Surely black prostitutes had to be removed as well. The *Nashville Daily Press* was adamant and called for a "summary and effectual remedy":

> *Unless the aggravated curse of lechery as it exists among the negresses of the town is destroyed by rigid military or civil mandates, or the indiscriminate expulsion of the guilty sex, the ejectment of the white class will turn out to have been productive of the sin will was intended to eradicate…No city…has been more shamefully abused by the conduct of its unchaste female population, white or black, than has Nashville for the past… eighteen months…We trust that, while in the humor of ridding our town of libidinous white women, General Granger will dispose of the hundreds of…black ones who are making our fair city a Gomorrah.*[69]

There is no indication, however, that black prostitutes were rounded up or exiled as their white sisters had been. In fact, while Nashville's streets were soon considered so safe that "the young ladies and matrons can resume their…walks and pilgrimages," at least two "bawdy houses" remained in the city. While the editors of the *Daily Press* were pleased at the "decampment of the 'wayward daughters,'" the prostitutes, under military guard, were on their way back to Nashville.[70]

The steamboat left Nashville for Louisville, Kentucky, on July 8, but authorities there refused to let the cargo of "ill-famed women" land. The same result was repeated at Cincinnati, Ohio, and Covington and Newport, Kentucky. Rumor held that the original order sending the prostitutes on their excursion had been revoked in Washington. The embarrassing fact that a government ship had been employed to carry the prostitutes resulted in the

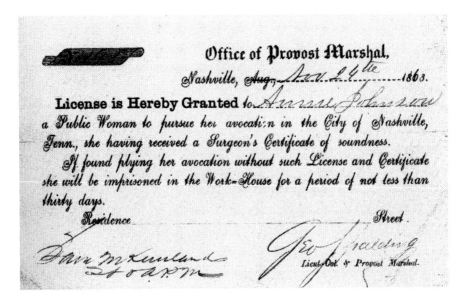

Prostitute's license, Nashville. *From Thomas P. Lowery's* The Story the Soldiers Wouldn't Tell *(2012).*

"very great grief of the army." The *Daily Press* was shocked and wished to send the women to Salt Lake City because "they'd make admirable latter day saints, and old Brigham would shout gloriously at their conversion."[71] Nevertheless, by August 4, the damaged *Idahoe* had returned, and the prostitutes were back in Nashville "to resume their former modes of life."[72]

Recognizing the exile's failure, Provost Marshal Spalding conceived a system of frequent medical inspection and licensed—and therefore legal—prostitution. His plan consisted of four parts. First, a license would be issued to each prostitute and a record kept of her address. Second, a surgeon would conduct weekly medical examinations; healthy women received a health certificate, while any diseased women were sent to a hospital for treatment. Third, a special hospital for contaminated prostitutes was to be established, and each prostitute would pay a fifty-cent weekly tax for its upkeep. Fourth, "all public women found playing their vocation without a license and health certificate" would be "incarcerated in the workhouse for…thirty days."[73] In addition to the prostitutes' hospital, a soldiers' "Syphilitic Hospital" would be established later. According to Dr. R. Wallace, stationed in Nashville, "this is the first time and place that anything of this kind [the licensed prostitutes system] has been in our country." The hospital for prostitutes was located in the North Market

Soldiers' Syphilitic Hospital, Nashville. *Hoobler Collection, Tennessee State Library and Archives.*

Street (now Second Avenue) mansion of Catholic Bishop Miles, while the soldiers' hospital was located at the Hynes High School at the intersection of Summer and Linds Streets (now Fifth and Jo Johnston Avenues).[74]

By January 1864, there were 300 licensed prostitutes and 60 cases of venereal disease reported among them. By early February, the *Daily*

Press reported that $2,879.40 had been collected in fees, which "upon the whole…may be regarded as a pretty good business." In April, the number of licensed prostitutes in Nashville was put at 352, while 92 cases of venereal diseases were treated. By June 30, a total of 994 cases had been admitted to the female hospital. Within a year of its initiation, 456 white and 50 black prostitutes had been registered. Writing in October 1864, Dr. Wallace claimed that soon after it opened, "the Syphilitic Hospital was so full…that the other hospitals had to retain that class of patients instead of transferring them."[75]

This novel preventative experiment also had some interesting social as well as medical consequences. As seen here, the number of registered prostitutes grew in occupied Nashville. This was partially because of what might be termed as better working conditions. Many of the increased number of public women had been "drawn to Nashville from northern cities by the comparative protection from venereal disease which its license system afforded." The prostitutes gladly showed their certificates to clients, while the women were protected from charlatans and quacks when seeking medical help. Additionally, the appearance and manners of the city's public

Nashville Cyprian's Hospital. *Hoobler Collection, Tennessee State Library and Archives.*

Office of Provost Marshal,
MEDICAL DEPARTMENT,
Nashville, Tenn., Dec. 20 : 1863

I Certify *that I have made a personal examination of* Bettie Duncan, *and find her free from contagious venereal diseases.*

Bay. C. Depot.

W. M. Chambers
Surgeon U. S, Vols.

PROVOST MARSHAL'S OFFICE,
NASHVILLE, TENN., _____, 1863.

Provost Orders, No. 21 :

All Public Women in the City of Nashville are hereby ordered to report at the Provost Marshal's Office before the 20th day of August, 1863.

On presentation of Surgeon's Certificate and payment of Five Dollars [$ 5:00] they will receive License for the practice of their profession.

All such Women found doing business after the 20th day of August, inst.. without such Certificate and License, will be arrested and incarcerated in the Work House for a period not less than Thirty Days.

By command of

GEO. SPAULDING, Lieut. Col. and Provost Marshal.

Brig. Gen. R. S. GRANGER.

(*Top*) Prostitute Bettie Duncan was issued this Weekly Certificate of Health on December 30, 1863, by the U.S. Army, signed by Dr. William M. Chambers. (*Bottom*) All Nashville prostitutes were notified that they must register and be examined or face thirty days' confinement. *National Archives, courtesy of Michael Musick.*

Official prostitution papers, Nashville. *From Thomas P. Lowery's* The Story the Soldiers Wouldn't Tell *(2012).*

women improved. When the system inspection and licensing began, most prostitutes "were exceedingly filthy in their persons and apparel and obscene and coarse in their language," a condition that "soon gave place to cleanliness and propriety."[76]

This was not entirely true, if what could best be called "Lady Godiva's Ride" in Nashville in September 1864 can be taken as evidence. It demonstrated that while the medical aspects of prostitution had been curbed to an extent, its bawdiness had not.

> On Thursday...the good citizens of Cherry Street, from Cedar to Broad... were treated to a sight so...insufferably disgusting, that it would be allowed no mention in our columns, were it not to call...the...law...to prevent the repetition of a similar occurrence. A fleshy...fille de joie, whose sense of modesty seemed wholly to have been merged in the large development of her physical charms, entirely nude from her waist heavenward, in an open hack, drove rapidly up Cherry Street. She was attired in a deep red dress, a jaunty hat trimmed with red...she reminded us of a conflict of arms in the ocean of blood. As she passed the Maxwell Barracks, the hundreds of soldiers...set up a lusty and continuous admiration...better...imagined than described... There may be a pleasure to these frail daughters of humanity in thus airing in the grateful evening air, but it is a pleasure we would fain believed shared in by none other than themselves...we think that the women who thus exposes to, and pollutes the public view with her disgusting nudeness, should be fined and punished to the full extent of the law.[77]

Public nudity aside, the medical purveyor for the U.S. Army in Nashville, H.R. Fletcher, who was also in charge of the hospital for prostitutes, made this appraisal of the system on August 15, 1864:

> It is not supposed that a system hastily devised, establishment for the first time on this continent...should be other than imperfect. We have no Parisian "Bureau des Moeurs," with its vigilant police...This much...is to be claimed, that after the...forcible expulsion of the prostitutes had... utterly failed, the more philosophic plan of recognizing and controlling an ineradicable evil has met with undoubted success.

While it was held incontestable that venereal disease had not been eliminated, it had been controlled. Regimental surgeons' reports indicated that because of the system, "the origin of the evil has been but to a small

Maxwell House, Nashville, showing detritus in streets. *Hoobler Collection, Tennessee State Library and Archives.*

extent traceable to this city." And no wonder, as it was by then common practice for officers to report both parties involved in any case of venereal disease. The offenders would then be sequestered for treatment, and thus the spread of venereal disease was ostensibly controlled.[78]

Memphis's wartime experience with prostitution is first noted in late August 1861, when the *Daily Appeal* announced in its columns that women were being arrested for "being inhabitants of houses of ill-fame." It was widely believed that the women were placed under arrest because of "the refusal of this class of this population to pay a monthly tax of fifty dollars per each house, to the city." It was decided by the city fathers that the tax was completely illegal, and it was abolished. The problem found no solution even after four months of Federal occupation when, in early September 1862, the authorities of Memphis were so alarmed at the presence of prostitutes that they took a strong-arm position and drove "the frail women out of the corporate limits of [the] city."

The problem persisted, and seven months later, the District Provost Marshal Lieutenant Colonel Melanchthon Smith laid down the law in the draconian Special Orders No. 13 on April 29, 1863:

If, after ten days from the date of this order any house of ill fame, kept for the purpose of prostitution and lewdness, is discovered in this District, the inmates thereof will be arrested and sent North, and their household furniture reported to the Commanding Officer for confiscation.

Any officer or soldier of the United States Army, who in this District should so far forget the respectability and dignity of his position, as to appear in places of the above named character, except on official duty, will, upon discovery, be reported with his name, and regiment, to the Commanding General.

Masters of steamboats are prohibited from bringing to this District and landing, as passengers, "prostitutes" or women of disreputable character. A violation of this order will subject the offender to arrest and fine. The local Provost Marshals in this District will see that these orders are enforced.[79]

Certainly these measures would rid the city of the "frail sisterhood" and cause a return to law and order in the Bluff City.

An editorial dealing with the closing of houses of ill fame appeared in the *Memphis Daily Appeal*. It recognized that there was no denying the notorious "fact…that our city at the present time is a perfect bee hive of women of ill fame." Public omnibuses had become theirs "by right of conquest, and ladies fear to ride on them fearing to be classed with them." Steamboats plying between Memphis and other cities to the north "have not the same respectability that characterized them in former years." In fact, Memphis morality had, furthermore, declined "from importation of lewd women from the North, [and] is almost at a discount." Incredibly, it was not uncommon for "that class of beings," wearing men's clothing (civilian as well as military), to be observed "in broad daylight, to the infinite satisfaction of the women and the great annoyance of respectable people."[80] District Provost Marshal Lieutenant Colonel Melanchthon Smith's order was applauded as the only way to stop the public health nuisance and moral affront.

Yet the predicament refused to go away. Only a month later, on May 18, 1863, Corporal George Hovey Cadman, Thirty-ninth Ohio Volunteer Infantry, left a vivid account of the chaos caused by Memphis prostitutes in a letter to his wife:

We reached Memphis by six P.M. [May 12]…When we arrived in Memphis our trouble began. Women and Whisky are plentiful here, and the men had been so long debarred from both that it did not take them long to raise Hell generally. Never did I see a such a scene before in my life, and hope to God I never may again, for some day in spite of all the Endeavors of the Colonel who did his utmost to preserve discipline, the Camp was one wild scene of Debauchery. One company got all its men in the [Irving] Block but three. Our men were not quite as bad as that, but the biggest part were drunk, in fact drunkenness was the order of the day, so you may form some idea of what the Camp was like, and with some Hundreds of the most abandoned women in the world to add their evil influence...Even now women come to the very Guard line with their bodies strung round with Whisky under their Clothes to sell themselves and a bottle of liquor for a Dollar. For the first few nights we could get no sleep for the cursing of the men [and] screaming of women and the firing of pistols outside the Camp.[81]

An editorial in the *Memphis Bulletin* in August echoed Cadman's observations. Under the title "Sinks of Pollution" the column claimed:

Our city is yet young in years, and her annals have not as yet been stained with any particularly marked locality for thieves and prostitutes...A few days since, a woman...was arrested of permitting a disorderly house to be found under her control. The woman was fined ten dollars and costs, and was thereupon discharged, to repeat the offense. We know there never has been a community so large as this where there were not such sinks of vileness; but we think that measures might be taken to render their bad influence less powerful.[82]

It was clear that the brawny approach would not bring about the desired effect. About a year after the Nashville experiment had been implemented, initial moves were made in Memphis to replicate it. Prostitution was still a problem, especially on the north side of Beale Street, where "the demimonde reigns supreme." Moreover, circumstances in Memphis made the imposition of a system of legal and licensed prostitution easier. Special Order No. 70, issued by General C.C. Washburn, placed the city under martial law on July 2, 1864. The entire municipal government was suspended, while military officers replaced municipal officers. Lieutenant Colonel Thomas H. Harris, and later Captain Richard Channing, served as mayor. The idea was to form regulations for the "government of prostitutes...in Memphis." By August 2, the provisional military government had adopted a resolution authorizing Harris to take action. After being approved throughout the chain of command, the system was initiated on September 30, 1864.[83]

General C.C. Washburn. *Library of Congress.*

According to a "Private Circular" that was intended for the information of women only: all prostitutes were to report to the registry office at 21 Union Street. "All women...in the city...living in boardinghouses, singly or as kept mistress" now had to "be registered and take out weekly certificates." Women living with responsible citizens of "good character" were exempt from weekly examinations. A fee of $2.50 was charged for a medical examination and a certificate, and provisions were made for house calls. Once a medical certificate was issued, a $10.00 registration fee was required. Every woman practicing prostitution in Memphis had until October 10 to comply. All monies thus received were to be used to support the newly established "private female wards" in the new City Hospital on the corner of Exchange Street and Front Row. These wards were for registered prostitutes only, and they were permitted admittance "at any time for any disease...free from any cost or charge whatever."

The army restrictions went beyond registration, however, and strictly forbade all prostitutes in Memphis from "'street walking,' soliciting, stopping, or talking with men on the streets; buggy or horseback riding for pleasure through the city in daylight; wearing a showy, flash [*sic*] or immodest dress in public; any language or conduct in public which attracts attention; visiting the public squares, the...theatre, or other resort of Ladies."[84]

According to City Hospital physician A. Gregg's report for February 1865, twenty-eight women remained in the hospital since January, while fifteen had been admitted since the beginning of the month. A total of forty-two women had been treated and fourteen discharged, while three women had died.[85]

Mayor Channing also reported in February that 134 women had been registered as prostitutes, 110 of whom lived in the city. Among these were 92 boarders, four kept mistresses and fourteen housekeepers. "The inmates of all public houses," reported Channing, "and all other white cyprians" were also catalogued. A total of $6,428.65 had been collected in various fees, with $2,535.16 spent on female hospital ward expenses, leaving a balance of $3,893.49. Since all the provost marshal's former efforts to suppress prostitution in Memphis had failed, as they had in Nashville, Mayor Channing realized that even though the system did not eliminate prostitution, it discouraged it and controlled its worst consequences.[86]

The numbers of prostitutes had grown with the increase of soldiers. While venereal diseases were the army's chief cause of concern in this situation, prostitution itself had unsettling effects on native morals as well. The unusual circumstance of civil war created a health problem that only martial authority could police adequately. Although the particulars of the fates of these two cities' experiments in social control and disease prevention are imprecise, it is clear that they were abandoned soon after hostilities ceased. The January 1865 report of Nashville surgeon William M. Chambers summarized a pattern that must have also occurred in Memphis: "The prostitutes complain that they are not making much money now because of the scarcity of troops around the city. These women are rapidly leaving in all directions, some profess to be going home, while others are looking for situations where money can be obtained wherewith to bedeck and bedizen themselves."[87]

Yet for the first time in American civil, military and urban history, successful efforts were made to control venereal diseases through the establishment of medically monitored and legalized prostitution. Justified as military necessities, the U.S. Army Medical Department's action to eradicate venereal diseases through the forced expulsion of prostitutes failed. Even though the cause-and-effect relationship between bacteria and infection was unknown, the army responded deftly and recognized that regulation through social control would maintain the health and effectiveness of its soldiers. The veiled mêlée in Tennessee's Civil War history was a victory in both medical and moral terms and illustrates the variety of experience in that conflict.

Chapter 3

THE STRUGGLE FOR PUBLIC HEALTH IN CIVIL WAR MIDDLE TENNESSEE CITIES

Significant events and names in Tennessee's Civil War history are well known and well chronicled. Dramatic stories of the Battles of Fort Donelson, Shiloh and Stones River and wartime biographies of famous Confederate and Federal generals have monopolized scholars' and readers' attention. In the past two decades, scholars have exposed a previously unheralded field of study of military health and hospitals in Tennessee cities during the war. Yet these are focused tightly on hospitals, surgical procedures, malnutrition and the organization of army medical services.[88] Save for one study examining the dilemmas of venereal infection and prostitution in Tennessee and the U.S. Army Medical Corps' solution to that public health and social problem,[89] the subject of public health in the Volunteer State during the war has been overlooked. This is largely due to the fact that, until recently, there has been no centralized body of evidence to consult.[90] While evidence focuses principally (but not exclusively) on Nashville during the Union occupation, some evidence reveals that the problems of filth and disease were closely related to the lack of any sanitary activity in other venues.

Nashville became an important center for logistical, supply and medical activities during the conflict, and the United States Army occupied it shortly after the fall of Fort Donelson in February 1862. It would not be surprising, then, to expect that most of the evidence available about public health issues would relate to it. Where armies increased in population, it was nearly certain that pestilence and public health disorders would increase as well. The problems presented by public health issues were not anticipated by the Federal army in the City of Rocks, but it became a problem of significance in Nashville. Source materials are scarce, yet they reveal an aspect of Tennessee's Civil War history that has been overlooked in the all but ubiquitous search for combat narratives.

Only days before the fall of Fort Donelson, the *Clarksville Chronicle* commented on the continual stretch of rain unheralded for years. One result of the rain was that city streets were turned to muck. "The accumulated dirt and filth of some two years," pointed out the editor, "has been chemically rendered into slosh [*sic*], so that Franklin street is as terrible to one wanting to cross it, as Styx is to a ghost without Charon's fee."[91] The focus was more on convenience than pestilence, but the threat of "two years" of accumulated filth to public health was recognized.

Public health was a matter of some concern in Murfreesboro in March 1863. According to longtime resident John C. Spence, the occupying Federal Army of the Cumberland was receiving large droves of beef cattle after the battle of Murfreesboro. Whether healthy or sick, the livestock were kept in lots at various locations around the city. It required the slaughter of some fifty or sixty cattle per day to supply the army and its hospitals. According to Spence's diary:

> *They would drive out that number,* [then] *shoot them down. When butchered, it generally covered over a half acre of ground, the entrails, heads and feet, left lying there—so in the course of time several acres was covered in this way, and it began to get warm weather. The smell became very offensive.*
>
> *We began to be apprehensive that it would cause sickness, but as fortune would have it, the authorities took the matter in hand-dug pits, had the offensive* [offal] *collected up and thrown in and covered up. This caused the atmosphere to improve.*

In addition, the army commenced a system of street cleaning whereby "hands were set to work scraping up all the litter that was lying in the streets, gutters and corners and hauled it out of town." The city took on a "more cheerful and healthy appearance," according to Spence.[92]

Yet another source described the general health issues menacing Murfreesboro. In an entry in his diary, B.F. McGee of the Seventy-second Indiana Infantry reported on the hygienic conditions of the Army of the Cumberland then occupying Murfreesboro and environs:

Sickness in the regiment prevails to an alarming extent; average attendance at the sick call, 100, perhaps 100 more are not fit for duty. This army of 40,000 men is encamped on a space so small that it is utterly impossible to keep the camps clean. Thousands of dead horses, mules and offal of every description, literally cover the whole face of the earth inside our picket lines; and each emits a thousand stinks, and each stink different from its fellow. The weather for months has been almost one continual flood of rain, and now, as the sun comes up more nearly straight over us, and pours down his boiling rays on this vast, sweltering mass of putridity, the stinks are magnified, multiplied and etherealized until the man in the moon must hold his nose as he passes over this vast sea of filth.[93]

By November 1863, five months after the launching of the Middle Tennessee Campaign, smallpox had become rampant in Murfreesboro. It was apparently restricted to the large unvaccinated contraband population. "Some white persons caught the disease," according to John Spence, and "a few died with it." He further observed:

A great many negros have fallen victims to the disease. It is a great wonder the plague has not been of a more alarming nature, as there were such a large number of negros in from the country, fit subjects, one in ten who had been vaccinated, and it being almost impossible to keep them from mixing about through one another. They seem to be like rats, [and] are going at all times and places. The army had a hospital built for that purpose, on the bank of the river near the Nashville pike. At this place the cases were moved to as fast as they were found out, which is the cause of the disease being kept down. Being told by one of the negros, who had been sick there, said the Drs and nurses paid little attention, or cared, whether or not they got well… Says as soon as the breath was out, they would lay the dead outside of the door, sometimes lay there a day or two before they were moved or buried… Large numbers died.[94]

Conditions in Confederate-occupied Fayetteville, Lincoln County, apparently did not vary much from those in Murfreesboro or Nashville. A rare and brief paragraph in the *Fayetteville Observer* entitled "Clean Up" indicates a growing concern over public health problems:

We would respectfully refer the attention of the authorities, civil or military, or both, to the condition of the streets, allies [sic], etc., of Fayetteville.

Federal troops in formation in Nashville Public Square. *Hoobler Collection, Tennessee State Library and Archives.*

Dead hogs, mules, and horses may be found in the corporation or vicinity, on all sides in every state of decomposition. The air is thick with incipient disease, and unless a speedy purifying is resorted to, midsummer will again find the cholera, or some other fatal epidemic in our midst. In behalf of the citizens, we ask that our town may now have a thorough cleansing. The soldiers, we have no doubt, would unite in the request.[95]

It is not known if the Army of Tennessee took measures to mitigate the problem.

Public health disquiet was a matter of anxiety for municipal and military authorities in Nashville as well. The spring of 1863 seems to have been a shared time for urban public health initiatives. Orders issued by the inspector general's office on March 16, 1863, required owners and occupants of businesses and dwelling houses to "have the streets, alleys and backyards adjoining their respective houses thoroughly cleaned." By late April, it was announced that an inspection "by proper authorized persons" of the work accomplished was to be executed. Brigadier General J.D. Morgan warned that "anyone found to have neglected to obey the Order will be severely punished."[96]

Nashville street scene. Note the open sewer and soiled streets. *Hoobler Collection, Tennessee State Library and Archives.*

In the meantime, Federal hospital authorities had contracted a sewer system from Hospital No. 9 to the Cumberland River, "through which flows all the waste water from every part of the hospital." This was said to have a cleansing and healthful effect on the hospital and its patients.[97] That the open sewer might be a prime factor for infecting the river and pose a health hazard to thousands seems hardly to have been a consideration.

Regardless, by the time the hot weather arrived in June, Mayor John Hugh Smith recognized that "the health of the city demands that it should

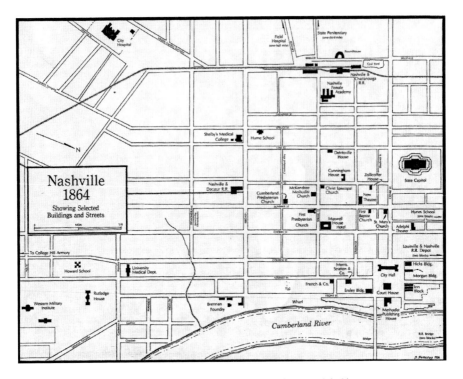

Map of Nashville, 1864. *Hoobler Collection, Tennessee State Library and Archives.*

be thoroughly cleansed." His public health notice spelled out a policy in which all filth or nuisances found on the premises of private citizens were to be removed "to the streets or alley and placed in heaps so the same may be hauled away by Government wagons furnished by Gen. Granger, Commander of the Post." Premises would be inspected and the city's nuisance law enforced. Reinforcing the idea that public health was both a military and civic responsibility was the aggressive threat that "[i]f the enforcement of civil law fails to effect the object, a more expeditious remedy may be applied."[98]

On July 9, 1863, the *Nashville Dispatch* commented on an advance copy of the report of the city agent of the pest house, Spencer Chandler. The incidence of smallpox was, according to statistics, on the decline, from eighteen cases to seven among whites and eighteen to sixteen among blacks. The figures for the African American population were troubling, however, showing that overall the disease was still virulent. Chandler was a qualified judge of such public health threats, and he feared "an increase not only of small pox, but of other diseases, among the blacks, unless some measures be adopted by the civil or military authorities, or both, to place the contrabands in healthy encampments, with guards and overseers to see after their health and morals." As the newspaper pointed out, there was another challenge to public health emanating from the contraband population, which was "scattered over the city and suburbs, and are crowded together by dozens and fifties [*sic*], many of the men living in idleness, some by thieving, a large number of the women by prostitution, and all in filth, breeding disease, which will spread like wildfire over the city. So barefaced are these black prostitutes becoming, that they parade the streets, and even the public square, by day and night."[99]

Public health problems were not limited to disease or poor sewerage only. In late July 1863, the editor of the *Nashville Dispatch* complained that the city had "more mean dogs and cats than any city of the same size was ever cursed with." It was practically impossible for anyone to walk the streets at night without kicking a few rats in his path, and "if he but imitate the bark of a dog, in two minutes from twenty to a hundred dogs will rush from their hiding places, and woe be to the smallest cur which happens amongst them. Night is made hideous with their cries of barking, and they finally crawl into the several holes, and the rats again hold a carnival among themselves." One man who owned some sixteen dogs "and an infinite number of cats" was nevertheless plagued by rats and complained that not only was "his house is eaten up by the rats, one of his cats had been recently killed by the vermin and his family was in constant danger of a rat attack." Perhaps the problem could be solved with a "rat hunter" whose duties would include shooting all "worthless dogs and cats on the premises, and then commence with traps and every device with human ingenuity has devised." Dogs and cats had a duty to perform to society, and all canine and feline pets should be made to perform duties to society, just as horses and mules did.[100] This seemed hardly a serious suggestion to controlling the exceptionally virulent rodent problem in Nashville.

In the late summer of 1863, what might have been a successful record of improvements in Nashville's public health were betrayed by the unsavory question, "Shall we be stunk to death?" Abundant rains had lately helped "purify our devoted city and save us from pestilence," but the recent drought called for some plan to rid the streets and alleyways of "the contaminating filth that spreads its vomitivie [*sic*] quintessence into every particle of space, [that] we shall not long have a corporal's guard on the healthy list." Nashville, long having a reputation "for cleanliness and hygeian [*sic*]," was now in the midst of a wave of miasmas and horrible odors. Why was there no board of health in Nashville? Weren't the city fathers aware of the problem? Didn't they ever

> *pass along near the Maxwell house, or any other of the perfumed localities, before breakfast, or after tea, when every thing is still. If they do, and inhale the delectable effluvium without being staggered and having a hurried desire to "cast up" all superfluous nourishment, they are proof against almost anything—they need not be "copper-bottomed" or "iron-clad." If we are to submit to the exhalations from dirty cellars and back premises, another month, all the good-smelling extracts ever compounded by the great Lubin[101] would fail to restore our nasal organs to their natural functions, nor would all of the Plantation Bitters in the country bring back our appetites. Shall we endure these unnatural sacrifices? That's the question. Shall we be stunk to death? That's another question.[102]*

If the corporation was not competent to carry out the vital job, no doubt General Granger should assume the task and "step into Doctor Butler's boots and clean out Nashville on the same admirable plan that New Orleans was redeemed from disease and death. Action! action! action!"[103]

Thus far, measures taken to improve public health in Nashville had not, despite the best intentions, proven successful. In a lengthy article by "SCALPLE," the *Daily Press* warned:

> *Yes the enemy is upon us; are even here now marching up our streets in solid columns, garrisoning our fortifications and throwing a guard into each farm and many of our houses; binding with chains not easily to be broken, a large portion of the residents, both citizens and soldiers; slaughtering without remorse, the old and young; the strong man at arms and the feeble woman; even the little child does not escape his power. Lawrence [sic] is invaded at our very doors. Yes, more than invaded, in awful distress, in panic, in these consequences death.[104]*

No, it wasn't the Confederate army but rather a legion of maladies—including malaria, typhoid, typhus, smallpox, septicemia,[105] gangrene, venereal diseases and dysentery—that were ensconced in Nashville. Public health matters were seriously awry in Nashville, where no one could walk "up Church Street, on the sidewalk, by the barracks, without holding his breath." Adding yet more authority to this claim, "SCALPLE" wrote, "even old boatmen are sickened by the horrid stench of the river

Nashville street scene, showing the offal pushed to the middle of the street. *Hoobler Collection, Tennessee State Library and Archives.*

[and]…the streets are the filthiest of any in the world, Constantinople not excepted." Not a day passed in which soldiers and citizens did not die from disease. There was fear that pestilence would find its way into the public market and the suburbs.[106] A correspondent for the *New York Times* concurred, writing that Nashville's "streets even surpass those of New York in accumulated filth, dirt and garbage, and under this tropical sun, steam with odious exhalations."[107]

The fault, it was believed, lay in the army's pass system, which allowed diseased people into the city. "SCALPLE" pointed out the "history of the Murfreesboro contract;[108] the fawning and…the whole history of various transactions in this department...which will account for the reason that the name of 'Grainger' [*sic*] has no angelic sweetness to his ear." Was the important work of public health the responsibility of the military or municipal authorities? "Let the responsible parties see to it. If they do not the people will see to them."[109]

Smallpox presented a dramatic threat to public health, and while there were some doubts in civilian medical and municipal circles about the logistics and propriety of taking forceful measures to protect public health, the military did not share those misgivings. Perhaps the best example can be found in General Orders No. 44, issued on November 24, 1863. By its provisions, the assistant medical director of the army forced the vaccination not just on military personnel but on citizens as well. Mayor Smith concurred. To facilitate this important medical prophylactic, army medical officers would be in attendance daily from 2:00 p.m. to 4:00 p.m. at the Alderman's Room in the Market House, on the Public Square, at Fire Engine House No. 3 and on Cherry Street in South Nashville. "Gratuitous vaccination will be afforded all these depots." The matter was deadly serious, and were any citizen to disobey the order, they would be subjected to a fine or to banishment north of the Nashville district's military lines. Commanding officers were ordered to see that their men were promptly vaccinated.[110]

Leaving a sense of fuming morality out of the question, Chandler's report noted that wherever a case of smallpox was found among contrabands, they lived overcrowded in a slum house. The editor of the *Dispatch* asked pointedly, "How many of these inmates of a filthy den have contracted the disease? Among how many others will they spread it? How long [a] time will elapse before it breaks out in camps, or in hospitals? (for many of the occupants of these dens spend their days in hospitals). These are questions to be reflected upon seriously by our City Fathers, if they would preserve the health of the city."[111]

Concurrently with the hazard of smallpox, a military order had just been received the day before notifying all white prostitutes to leave Nashville without delay. If this public health tactic was good for them, "why not issue a similar order against the blacks? If military necessity demands the removal of the first, it certainly will require the latter, if the police and our own eyes are to be believed."[112]

Indeed, Nashville had become notorious for its "Smokey Row," the de facto red-light district of the city. The incidence of venereal disease among the troops, and no doubt the civilian population, was so alarming that in July military authorities conducted a prostitute pogrom and sent the women via steamboat to Cincinnati. That city refused them, and within two months, most of the "Cyprians" had returned to Nashville. Seeing that expulsion would not protect soldiers' and public health, the military medical department in Nashville initiated a system of frequent and regular health inspections for prostitutes in an effort to reduce disease in the army. If found free of disease, the prostitute paid for a license and was allowed to continue her profession. It was the first licensed system of prostitution in the United States.[113]

A number of bordellos there created a "perfect pest house." It was common knowledge that "hundreds of soldiers and some hospital workers frequent those houses." One house of ill repute on College and Criddle Streets had at least two sex workers who were smallpox patients, as well as "*some other girls.*" Knowing this, the editor of the *Dispatch* asked, "Are such things calculated to increase or diminish the spread of small pox? Imagine an inmate of one of our hospitals spending one night with two small-pox patients, and the next day and night in a hospital!"[114]

On January 24, 1864, Brigadier General R.S. Granger issued General Orders No. 4. All cases of smallpox, soldiers or citizens, were to be "promptly reported the Acting Assistant Surgeon A.D. White at his office in the Bostick house, a large brick building on the Charlotte Pike." From that point, all bona fide cases were to be conveyed to "the small-pox camps and treated." Granger justified the necessity of this action on the grounds that the "unchecked spread of this disease necessitates this regulation, which will be strictly enforced.[115]

There was little authorities could do to quell smallpox, and by February 1864, its occurrence in Nashville was alarming. The number of cases of the disease was being recorded. The two bagnios on Criddle and College Streets contained cases of smallpox, and large numbers of soldiers and hospital employees were known to frequently spend time in them, day and night. It seemed no wonder, then, that 137 soldiers had been infected with the pox. There had been no effort made to prevent the spread of the disease among the contraband, and this accounted for the upsurge. The increase in smallpox cases among contraband had expanded from 76 in November 1863 to 219 in January 1864, and that figure did not include those in the military hospitals.

INCREASE IN THE INCIDENCE OF SMALLPOX IN NASHVILLE,
NOVEMBER 1863–JANUARY 1864

Admitted	November '63	December '63	January '64
Citizens	23	66	87
Soldiers	47	86	137
Contrabands	76	173	219
Total	**146**	**325**	**443**

This report presented an alarming picture of dramatic and dangerous increase of smallpox, and the municipal authorities' attention was drawn to it. In the early part of December 1863, Mr. Spencer Chandler presented a report to the city council, making some rational proposals, and he urged immediate action to protect the public health. The report was referred to the Pest House Committee, but nothing whatever was done. "Almost every street in the city in infected," according to a newspaper report, and "almost every negro den has its patient, and yet we hear of no measures for its amelioration—no active, vigorous measures, such as should be put forth for the prevention of its further spreading."

The pest house report for the month of January demonstrated the veracity of Chandler's claims:

NASHVILLE PEST HOUSE REPORT FOR JANUARY 1864

Number in hospital as per last report	349
Since admitted citizens	87
Since admitted soldiers	137
Since admitted contrabands	219–443
Total number treated	792
Discharged	107
Died	114
Escaped	2–223 [*sic*]
Remaining in Hospital	559

There were, at that time, nine pest houses/hospitals in Nashville, including smallpox hospitals and surgeons' quarters: "Dr. Watson's house, Langdon's, Beech's, Ed. Smith's, two houses belonging to Whiteman, the old Pest House on the river, and the Bostick house on the Charlotte Pike, as headquarters. J.B. McFerrin's house, in Edgefield, is also used as a pest-house."[116]

By April 1864, the menace was nonetheless virulent. Elvira Powers was a novitiate nurse who volunteered to work at the Nashville smallpox hospital. Her job entailed caring for patients in "two divisions of tents at the Small Pox Hospital." She described in her diary the particular hospital at which she had volunteered to work as a "most disagreeable place, as there are so few who are willing to take it." She continued:

> *The Hospital is about a mile out from the city, and near Camp Cumberland. It consists of tents in the rear of a fine, large mansion which was deserted by its rebel owner. In these tents are about 800 patients—including convalescents, contrabands, soldiers and citizens. Everything seems done for their comfort which can well be, with the scarcity of help. Cleanliness and ventilation are duly attended to; but the unsightly, swollen faces, blotched with eruption, or presenting an entire scab, and the offensive odor, require some strength of nerve in those who minister to their necessities. There are six physicians each in charge of a division. Those in which I am assigned to duty are in charge of Drs. R. & C. There is but one lady nurse here, aside from the wives of three surgeons—Mrs. B., the nurse, went with me through the tents, introduced me to the patients and explained my duties.*[117]

Martial authorities, however, had a clear idea of who was responsible: city authorities. They had not done an adequate job in protecting public health in Nashville. In late January 1864, Brigadier General R.S. Granger launched the military's draconian response to the challenges to public health. Noting the utter failure of the municipal authorities to enforce public health regulations to protect the well-being and lives of soldiers and citizens, he ordered each occupant of every house in the city to "daily sweep or scrape clean the pavement of sidewalk in front of his building." This task was to be completed before 9:00 a.m. Thereafter, on announced days, each occupant was to clean to the middle of the street in front of his dwelling "collecting the sweepings into piles, to be carried away by Government wagons." A fine twice as high as one charged by the municipal authorities would be levied by the provost marshal for neglecting the order. If the fine were not paid within a week of being imposed, some of the offender's property would be sold at public auction until the sum was realized. A commissioned officer whose special duty it was to report any neglect or violation of the order was detailed to superintend the policing of the cleanliness of the city streets.[118]

The difficulties encountered by the municipal authorities in trying to keep the avenues of Nashville clean stemmed from a number of factors. Firstly, it was common knowledge that in the winter months, it had been wholly impossible to do any street cleaning because the ground was frozen. Notwithstanding, while the ground had been frozen, Mayor Smith applied to military authorities for the necessary carts to be used for street cleaning purposes. The mayor was prepared to pay for them. There being no response, the mayor wrote to the authorities stating that the city had no carts and that none could be bought in Nashville, and he again asked for the military to provide the corporation "with the number requisite to remove the mud from the streets." The letter was then sent through the military bureaucracy, and on the twenty-fifth, army authorities promised to furnish any number required at any time and place the mayor might designate. Smith requested some eight carts and wished to have them delivered to the city street overseer on the twenty-sixth. Sadly, due to pressing military business, the carts were not delivered, and the street cleaning order was issued on the twenty-seven. Moreover, the mayor had advertised to pay the "highest price" weeks before for one hundred hands to do the work. A breakdown in communications between military and civil authority was largely at fault for the lack of action.[119]

Second, there was a severe shortage of labor resulting from the vicissitudes of Civil War. Traditionally, the streets of Nashville were cleaned and kept in order by workhouse criminals and slaves leased by the year, but now

> [o]ur slaves are all gone, and none can be hired. It is deemed almost a miracle to find a negro in the workhouse two hours after he is convicted of a misdemeanor; he is either liberated by order of some military official, or is enlisted in the army, and we hear no more of him until again caught engaged in crime; but the same course is again pursued, and he is again liberated. It is thus that the Street Overseer is frequently without hands, and seldom has more than a dozen or twenty at his command.[120]

The large amount of rock needed for macadamizing the streets was manufactured in the workhouse by white criminals, but lately, "before a criminal has time to make a second breath after reaching the workhouse, the recruiting officer pounces upon him, and he is liberated to enter the service of Uncle Sam." Even if they were to find themselves back in the workhouse, their stay was truncated once their officers freed them.[121]

Thus, there were contradictory and extenuating impulses at work preventing the consummation of the street cleaning public health initiative. On the one hand was the desire to improve public health, and on the other were the demands of the military and the shortage of labor caused by the war. The editor of the *Dispatch* asked that the mayor be given an opportunity to remedy the situation. "These facts we publish for the information of the military authorities, and in justice to our civic officers. With many of them we are perfectly familiar, and we believe to be perfectly true all we have above stated. Give the Mayor half a chance, and he will do justice to all alike, military and civilian."[122]

Dead animal carcasses continued to be a problem in Nashville. According to one newspaper report, "Large numbers of the carcasses of dead mules and horses are rotting upon the commons close by the corner of Summer and Crawford streets, filling the air with an intolerable stench, which is admirably calculated to increase the business of physicians and undertakers."[123]

All past attempts to deal with this predicament had failed. Perhaps a solution could be found in constructing a large furnace where animal carcasses could be burned. Objections that it would require excessive amounts of wood to fire the furnace weren't as burdensome as some proclaimed, and regardless, "the health of the city is worth more than all the wood that could possibly be consumed." Disappointingly, the established practice of burying dead animals "played out long ago." There seemed to be no better idea than the furnace, and the editor invited comments from readers.[124]

Since the city seemed incapable of action, the army took the initiative. Provost Orders No. 52 was issued by Provost Marshal Lieutenant Colonel John W. Horner on March 13, 1864, mandating the elimination of dead animals from the streets of Nashville. The practice of disposing of the carcasses of dead mules and horses within the city limits "in violation of all sanitary regulations" was strictly prohibited. According to Provost Marshal Horner, all "such dead animals will be hauled to a point on the river bank, below the Government corrals, and thrown into the river." Anyone leaving a dead animal either in or within half a mile of the city limits who neglected to have it hauled away "will be arrested and imprisoned." The editor of the *Dispatch* applauded the order as "very wholesome." Yet while clean streets might be wholesome, many were upset that street scraping continued on Passion Sunday. "It has been said for ages that 'cleanliness is *next* to godliness,' not to be preferred to it."[125]

On March 22, 1864, Captain William D. Chamberlain, chief of the military police at Nashville, issued Special Orders No. 76. His duties were to search all premises, alleys and outhouses and to give orders and directions involving the cleaning and maintenance of them. The order likewise provided that no impediment could be allowed on the pavements but rather should "be taken in as soon as delivered." For its part, the government would see to it that the streets were kept clean by sprinkling them daily. The prospect for a healthy summer seemed possible.[126]

Special Orders No. 76 was sweeping in its objective to improve public health. The civilian population of the city would find it to their individual and mutual interests to assist Chamberlain. The order consisted of seven parts:

I. That occupants of Stores, Restaurants and Dwelling Houses, will be required to clean their yards and cellars, and have the offal removed, within forty-eight hours from the date of this order. No garbage or dirt of any kind will be allowed, to accumulate on any premises within the city limits.

II. All dirt to be removed in barrels and boxes from the back yards and alleys by the persons occupying the same. No rubbish will be allowed to remain more than twenty-four hours without being removed.

III. Offal, the accumulation of restaurants, must be removed by the occupants each day (Sundays excepted) before 10 A.M. each day.

IV. Hereafter occupants of Stores and Houses will be required to have the rear of their premises clean, and the side walk swept before 9 A.M. each day.

V. Any violation of the above Order will be punished by a fine of Five Dollars ($5) to be collected by the Provost Marshal.

VI. As cleanliness is one of the first requisites to health, it is hoped the citizens will all in their power to assist in the moving of the first causes of disease. As soon as a sufficient number of carts can be procured, notice will be given, and the dirt and rubbish removed without cost to citizens.

VII. As it is my intention to remove all filth from the city proper, whether in the shape of dirt, rubbish, or deal animals; any information that would facilitate the above will be thankfully received and immediate action taken in the premises.

Wm. D. Chamberlain, Capt. and Chief of City Police.[127]

Adding additional vigor to the effort to improve public health, Brigadier General Granger appointed U.S. Army surgeon L.A. James, of the Fourth

Ohio Volunteer Cavalry, as the first acting health officer for Nashville on March 30.[128]

The work of scraping the streets continued in April, with the object of eradicating smallpox and pneumonia. The work was supervised by two military captains and "reviewed semi-occasionally by Gen. Wright."[129] Ironically, that same day, nurse Powers recorded in her diary that a "woman and a boy died in my division last night. The father, a soldier, wishes to take the child away, but was not permitted to do so or to see it, for fear of contagion. It is to be kept to see if the child has the disease." The boy, from Alabama, thought that he was getting better but died. She recorded a conversation she had with one of her civilian patients, who died a day later:

> "People die mighty easy here." I asked in what way, he meant. "Oh," he replied, "they'll be mighty peart-like, one minute, an' the next you know, they're dead!" This is true, and I find so many who were sent here with measles, recover from those, and die of small pox. Sixty cases of measles were sent to this hospital in one month, as I learn from the lips of the surgeon in charge himself, Dr. F. These are sent by the several physicians of Nashville. The fact itself speaks volumes, but to stay here and see its effects day after day in the poor victims of such ignorance, impress one with a sense of the importance by the medical faculty of distinguishing between the two diseases.[130]

Apparently, the tough measures taken by the military had an effect on the populace of Nashville, although perhaps not of the sort intended. While the citizens obeyed the public health orders in what might be interpreted as a passive-aggressive manner, the military could not live up to its end of the bargain. According to one source in early April:

> We are informed on authority that the mountains of dirt, ashes, filth, or what not, piled up in front of sundry houses, must be removed immediately at the expense of the owner or occupant of the house from whence it was exhumed, or the officers of the city government will indict the occupants for creating a nuisance. General Granger says he never contemplated having huge nuisances removed at the expense of Uncle Sam. We have warned you in time, reader; so look out for a notice to appear, and answer, etc., if your mud-piles are not removed this morning.[131]

Nashville's citizens were by this time thoroughly nonplussed in understanding their obligations with regard to the sanitary regulations laid down by the military authorities. Everyone seemed to have interpreted these orders to require them to place rubbish and ashes from their cellars, backyards and alleys in barrels and boxes on the streets in front of their businesses or premises, from whence they would be removed in government wagons. They complied with what they understood the orders to mean and now found the city authorities telling them that if they did not remove the rubbish, they were to be indicted for creating a nuisance. "The law is plain and explicit upon this point, and the citizens must remove the rubbish in front of their premises forthwith or take the consequences."

There were contradictions in the municipal ordinances and the military orders that would result in a doubling of fines. The solution to the public health conundrum was clearly to have either the military or municipal authorities enforce police and sanitary regulations in the city. The no-nonsense policy adopted by General S.A. Hurlbut in Memphis was thought to present a worthy model for emulation. In a speech to the city council on the seventeenth, he proclaimed that if they did not clean the city and take measures to improve its sanitary condition, he would impose military authority, abolish their power to collect taxes and do the work himself.[132] Within a week, it was noted that the "shovel brigade" was out in force, "going through its maneuvers with remarkable accuracy...These forces are intended to operate principally against Small Pox and Pneumonia, two desperate enemies of mankind generally."[133] Nashville Board of Aldermen minutes, however, demonstrate that no permanent board of health had been created by the municipal government.[134]

Some unanticipated threats to public health had not been legislated against. One example was the "outrageous nuisance" committed daily on "the bank of the [Cumberland] river at the foot of Church Street." There, literally hundreds of people customarily "perform the mysterious rights of the goddess Cloacina,[135] the thoughts of which makes one involuntarily hold his nose." Certainly, using the banks of the Cumberland River as a lavatory was neither sanitary nor conducive to public health, and the police were urged to oblige the offenders to "evacuate the premises."[136]

While public health was an arena for military initiatives, public authorities were reluctant to become involved in this important function. One positive result of the battle for public health was a growing recognition that urban governments must expand to preserve and maintain the health of Nashville. In 1867, the City of Nashville hired its first public health officer, Dr. Joseph

Jones,[137] a former Confederate army surgeon. While his tenure was fleeting, it is an indication that the necessity of maintaining public health had become a legitimate consideration of urban government. The recognition was slow, owing to undiscovered connections between germs as the cause of some diseases and a universally accepted *post hoc ergo propter hoc* construct that held that invisible and malodorous miasmas were the triggers for threats to public health. Certainly, the strains of martial occupation were not envisioned and could not have been planned for. Venereal diseases, open sewers, dead animals, swamps, mosquitoes, protozoan, sick contraband and disease-ridden army camps only exacerbated the situation. Ironically, it was the U.S. Army, the very source of most of the public health crises in middle Tennessee cities, that was the force that would attempt to jump-start sanitary measures. While the army medical actions were taken more to protect soldiers than civilians, they helped quell and prevent disease outbreaks nevertheless.

Chapter 4

THE INADVERTENT CONFEDERATE GUERRILLA LEADER

Colonel John M. Hughs, Twenty-fifth Tennessee Infantry

While the American Civil War is often portrayed as a series of large and decisive martial conflicts, it was also characterized by another, more vicious attribute played out on a much smaller but nonetheless bloody scale, namely guerrilla combat. Deriving its name from the small-scale attacks that Spanish civilians made on isolated groups of Napoleonic forces during the French occupation and Peninsular War of 1808–14, guerrilla warfare became an integral part of the American conflict. Those with opposing political views, or those with little but the prospect of pillage as motivation, joined forces and roamed the countryside foraging, attacking and murdering civilians, striking Federal forces and expropriating and destroying supplies, trains, houses and mills. They took prisoners and likewise burned houses or parts of towns to the ground.

It was ironically unique in the history of warfare in the Cumberland Plateau, in middle Tennessee, that a regular Confederate officer utilized undisciplined local manpower and guerrilla tactics to take the fight to maintain a resistance movement against the enemy. Confederate colonel John M. Hughs[138] found the role thrust on him in the autumn of 1863. His story is as worthy of attention during the sesquicentennial as are those of Nathan Bedford Forrest or narratives about the Battles of Shiloh or Stones River.

Before the war, Hughs kept a hotel in Livingston, Overton County, Tennessee.[139] As the conflict approached, he volunteered for the Twenty-fifth Tennessee Volunteer Infantry, rising to the rank of colonel in the regular Army of Tennessee. He was a seasoned veteran, having participated in the Battles of Fishing Creek,[140] Perryville[141] and Stones River (where he was wounded[142]), as well as the delaying action at Hoover's Gap, Tennessee.[143] Hughs, shortly after the Army of the Cumberland's successful middle Tennessee offensive, was ordered by General Braxton Bragg to Tennessee's Cumberland Plateau to enforce the Confederate draft and to round up deserters and stragglers on August 16, 1863. Within two days, he had advanced to middle Tennessee[144] with twenty men from the Twenty-fifth, carrying orders for Captain M.V. Amonett (Shaw's cavalry) to assist Hughs in collecting absentees.

His force was then stationed at Loudon, Tennessee, some ninety miles from the area where Hughs was to carry out his tasks. His men had to march on foot, which slowed the undertaking. Thus, nothing "was done in the way of our appropriate duty until the 25th of August, when, all being mounted, and Amonett's company having reported, we set to work." Within a few weeks, Hughs had arrested twenty deserters, then he heard rumors that Federal columns were moving through both Overton and White Counties, his immediate area of operations. Union columns were marching to Knoxville. Scouts reported that more enemy units were passing in considerable force, both via Sparta (White County) and Livingston (Overton County), and left him completely cut off from communication with the Army of Tennessee.[145] His small band of regulars was no equal to the vast Federal force.

Hughs hastily sought out an isolated place in the county[146] where he could safely ensconce his command. Several days were occupied in determining whether they could somehow return to the Army of Tennessee. The consensus was that it would be altogether too dangerous an enterprise, and Hughs was compelled to release the stragglers. He had but three options: hide, surrender or operate against the enemy. The Federal presence in the Cumberland Plateau had, according to Hughs, "greatly emboldened the Union tories," who were becoming troublesome, forming bands, robbing and murdering citizens and soldiers in the area. "To punish these villains," Hughs reported, "a little fighting was necessary."[147] And fighting he would have; small parties of the Unionist civilians and Federal soldiers were stationed throughout the environs, giving him a large and incomparable field of targets to attack and harass with hit-and-run tactics. It was not long before the ranks of his command had enlarged to more than one hundred officers and conscripts with little military experience. There were several other legitimate Confederate officers in the Cumberland Plateau carrying out orders similar to his. But they refused to cooperate with him, and Hughs was forced to rely on his own small command in all combat with the Federal forces. As future events unfolded, his "small command" would swell with disruptive and unruly guerrillas.[148]

Hughs wasted little time in carrying out his tactical attacks against "tory" bands and Federal soldiers. His first assault took place on September 6, 1863, when he attacked the rear of the Fourteenth Illinois Volunteer Infantry as it marched toward Knoxville. In two days, he attacked the notorious Union guerrilla leader "Tinker" Dave Beatty,[149] although he inflicted no casualties. Eight days later, Hughs's command attacked and, firing behind every rock and tree, harassed the Eleventh and Twenty-seventh Kentucky Mounted Infantries as they marched to Knoxville from Albany, Kentucky. It was a successful encounter, resulting in the capture of twenty-six prisoners "and 112 fine beef cattle."[150]

A newspaper report in September recounted how a guerrilla band of thirty-five led by Oliver Hamilton, recently menacing southern Kentucky and "probably under the command of Hughes," attacked the Louisville and Nashville railroad early on Wednesday morning (the sixteenth), setting fire to the Nolin bridge. Citizens extinguished the fire, and the paper's editor added, "The raid was too hazardous for the rebels, who are sometimes possessed with desperate courage, and proved an utter failure."[151] What is of more importance is that Hughs was already known as a competent guerrilla commandant.

On October 6, Hughs's ambitions expanded to the point that his command, after uniting with Oliver Hamilton's guerrilla band, attacked Glasgow, Kentucky. Major Samuel Martin, Thirty-seventh Kentucky Infantry, was surprised by the attack. His report of October 9, 1863, told how Hughs and his men were lucky when they attacked Glasgow because the Federal the provost guards were all asleep, except for those on duty at the guardhouse and patrols about town. As they charged directly into the fort, its few defenders fired their guns promptly at the raiders, killing one. Nevertheless, in a Civil War version of "shock and awe," the dash into camp was so swift that the Federals were thrown into confusion; in fact, being new recruits, they "were panic-stricken." Colonel Hughs demanded the Yankees' surrender. The Federal commander stubbornly notified the Confederate guerrilla leader that he would have to fight them if he wanted prisoners. Yet his men would not have been able to mount a defense, as they comically "were then running in every direction, many without their arms or clothes."

The Confederate guerrillas' booty included more than two hundred horses and attendant equipments, all the Federal military unissued clothing on hand and two wagons packed with merchandise and supplies. They destroyed what they couldn't take, burning commissary stores and a large building at the fort. They carried off about one hundred carbines and left thirteen wounded. Hughs's men also robbed $9,000 in citizens' savings from the bank and robbed one store of $400 worth of goods, not stopping until they had escaped with civilian horses and buggies to carry off their wounded.

Champ Ferguson, Confederate guerilla leader, while awaiting trial in 1865. *From* Frank Leslie's Illustrated Newspaper, *Tennessee State Library and Archives.*

An unsuccessful pursuit was made of Hughs's command. The guerrillas crossed Cumberland River into Turkey Neck Bend, and Hughs, hearing that he was being chased, passed on to Kittle Creek, where they stopped and paroled their 142 prisoners. After crossing the Cumberland River, they scattered. Reports about the number of guerrillas involved in the Glasgow raid varied from two hundred to ten.[152] Reports held that the guerrillas had been overtaken and that all that had been stolen was recaptured were false.[153]

Another result of the attack was the consternation and terror that it caused in southern Kentucky, between the Tennessee state line and Munfordville. Likewise was the cooperation, expansion and coalescing of previously independent guerrilla bands under the management of Hughs, including Oliver Hamilton and Champ Ferguson, all operating in the Tennessee Cumberland Plateau and southern Kentucky. Soon after Hughs's Glasgow raid, rumor spread like wildfire that the fortified guerrillas were threatening Lebanon, Kentucky, leading to citizens "preparing to leave for parts unknown, and our worthy Provost Marshal was decidedly excited." It was soon discovered that the threat was only a rumor, and life returned to normal.[154] Near Burksville, Kentucky, a "very highly respectable citizen" reminded the military authorities that the border counties needed protection. According to the citizen, "They should be protected against such rebel hellhounds as Hughes, Ferguson, Hamilton, & Co., and, also, against such Union hell hounds as Captain Coffel…I hope the military will send a few good troops in here and let them remain until they catch or drive off such scoundrels as I have mentioned. If they do not we are or shall be ruined."[155]

After the successful October raid on Glasgow, Hughs and his men sought refuge in Tennessee with a contingent of Champ Ferguson's force in the rugged environs of the solidly pro-Confederate town of Sparta in White County. Federal forces were, however, engaged in pursuit of Rebel guerrillas and irregulars. The Confederates had remained at ease in their camps for more than six weeks when they were surprised by the First Tennessee Cavalry, led by Colonel James P. Brownlow, son of the strident east Tennessee pro-Union journalist. Two separate skirmishes took place, although the dates vary according to the reports of Hughs and Brownlow. On November 24, the Federal commander split his force, approached on the three roads leading to Sparta and "had a skirmish on each road. I whipped Col. Murray's[156] force, killing 1 wounding 2 and capturing 10 men." One of these was a lieutenant in Ferguson's band. Intelligence indicated that the Rebels would not take the assault without retribution; a contingent of Hughs's force, along with his associates from Hamilton's, Daugherty's and Ferguson's camps, as well as others, gathered for a counterattack. Brownlow reported, "I will give them hell if they come, although their force is largely superior to mine." In response, Brownlow's commanding officer, Brigadier General Washington L. Elliott, immediately bolstered the First Cavalry with one hundred men from the Second Michigan Cavalry.

On November 26, Brownlow's scouts skirmished with guerrillas within two miles of their camp. They killed two and captured four guerrillas. In addition, the First Tennessee destroyed the extensive Confederate saltworks. Brownlow successfully thwarted the Rebels from burning the twenty "fine merchant mills" within ten miles of Sparta.[157] Actually, while there were guerrilla forces in the Sparta area, Hughs himself most likely was not there, as his report states that he was at Monticello, Kentucky.[158]

While Hughs was picking quarrels and winning laurels after the triumphant raid on Monticello, there was a clash back in Tennessee at the White County hamlet of Yankeetown on November 30. As Colonel Brownlow had it, Colonel Hughs's command—then consisting of Murray's, Hamilton's, Bledsoe's, Ferguson's, Daugherty's and other sundry guerrilla bands—attacked First Lieutenant Bowman of the First Tennessee while the Federals were conducting a reconnaissance. After a prolonged interval of skirmishing, Bowman drove the Confederate guerrillas across the Calfkiller River at a point two miles east of Yankeetown, killing four, wounding one and capturing five. Brownlow, with his reinforced task force, "went immediately to his assistance, and drove the enemy (numbering 500[159]) 8 miles, killing 9, and wounding between 15 and 20." Ominously, Brownlow added, "I would take no prisoners."[160] According to Hughs, who was not present at the Yankeetown defeat, the fight took place between his rear guard, under Captain R.S. Bledsoe, and a contingent of Brownlow's First Cavalry. According to Hughs, Brownlow lost thirteen killed, eight wounded and seven captured. The Confederate loss was five killed. He did not mention the settlement of Yankeetown or the rout across the Calfkiller River.[161]

Another significant partisan raid led by Hughs was the strike at Scottsville, Kentucky, on December 8, 1863. With a command of two hundred irregular volunteer horsemen, he attacked the town, swiftly capturing the place and, as in Glasgow a few weeks earlier, took its garrison, commanded by Captain Gilliam's company of the Fifty-second Kentucky Regiment, numbering but eighty-six men. Hughs also collected as booty "a considerable quantity of quartermaster and commissary stores, together with about 500 stand of small-arms and several hundred saddles, bridles, &c. The prisoners were paroled. My loss, 1 killed."[162] But there was more to the incident than Hughs's characteristically terse report specified.

"The Surrender of Scottsville—Gallant and Desperate Resistance— Rebel Outrages—The Town Plundered and Fired by the Guerrillas" read the headlines of one of the scarce newspaper reports covering the event.[163] Captain J. D. Gillum and his inadequate command of eighty-six of the Fifty-second Kentucky Mounted Infantry had been stationed to defend the town and environs for a seventy-five-mile circumference. It was in a section of the state that gave all military advantages to guerrillas. One source claimed that the guerrillas—numbered from four hundred to five hundred, commanded by Hughs and composed of contingents of Hamilton's and Daugherty's groups—attacked at night, "yelling like so many fiends broke loose from pandemonium." The men of the Fifty-second, however, did not quickly surrender, and although vastly outnumbered, they took refuge in the courthouse and fought the Rebel raiders for nearly an hour. They surrendered only after they had depleted their ammunition.

Colonel Hughs accepted Captain Gillum's capitulation and earnestly guaranteed that citizens' property would be unmolested "and that there would be no departure on their part from the rules of civilized warfare during their occupation of the town." The assurance broke down shortly after the Confederates actually took over the town.

Soon after achieving complete control of the town, the already attenuated discipline deteriorated, and the "usual pillaging and robbery of stores and residences commenced." Everything of value that they could lay their hands on was taken. Not satisfied and in violation of men's pledge, the clerk's office was broken into and the public documents mutilated and destroyed, after which the courthouse was set on fire.

The guerrillas broke open the jail and released two of their comrades. Although they made a concerted effort to burn the jail, they were "thwarted in their hellish design by the united efforts of our soldiers and citizens," related one account.[164]

One man's triumphant raid into enemy territory was another's distressed ruin. Leaders such as Hughs were interested in fighting the enemy, directly if possible, not in plunder and fire. His hope was to maintain the hold of the Confederacy in the Kentucky-Tennessee Cumberland Plateau region. Yet his options were limited largely to ensure victory by fighting inferior enemy concentrations and to prey on civilian targets while leading a largely unprofessional martial force. The latter only increased terror of and hatred for the Confederacy, while the former led to increasingly aggressive Federal anti-guerrilla efforts.

Demonstrating that he could be more a soldier than a guerrilla, Hughs found an opportunity to reinforce his reputation as a regular military commander and combatant. On December 15, near Livingston, Tennessee, with a portion of his command totaling fewer than one hundred, he attacked a detachment of the Thirteenth Kentucky Mounted Infantry, numbering 250 men. In the action that followed, Hughs's command "succeeded in whipping and driving them out of the State, a distance of 18 miles, killing and wounding several and capturing 6. My loss, 2 wounded."[165] Here Hughs can be viewed as the defender of Confederate citizens, a liberating knight in the southern belief in a tradition of chivalry.

Circumstances continued to keep Hughs in middle Tennessee throughout the winter and early spring. During this time, however, he did not raid unsuspecting towns and villages but rather initiated small-scale battles against an enemy both more numerous and professional (if not callous). Even so, he did not shy away from a fight and earned the approbation of his Yankee foe.

The unusually frigid weather of January 1864 circumscribed Hughs's ambitions to carry the struggle to the enemy. When he was joined by Major Bledsoe, another Army of Tennessee officer, he was able to engage in hunting down the tories and Union bushwhackers. On February 14, he was able to divide his command, half under Major Bledsoe in White County, while Hughs remained in Overton County. Freezing weather notwithstanding, Hughs reported that "a great many tories and bushwhackers were killed and some slight engagements with the enemy occurred."[166]

Hughs was quickly in an engagement with Colonel William B. Stokes, Fifth Tennessee Cavalry, on the fifteenth. Stokes's command had been engaged in anti-guerrilla activities in middle Tennessee beginning in February 1864.[167] As early as February 1–7, 1864, his command conducted a scout in White and Putnam Counties, areas of guerrilla concentration. In that action, he covered the territory in an irregular quadrangle encompassing Sparta, Yankeetown, Cookeville, Rock Island and Lancaster. At the conclusion of the scout, Stokes reported that he had engaged with small bands of bushwhackers, taking twelve prisoners and killing seventeen "of the worst men in the country."[168] Stokes had not yet come upon Hughs's command. On February 15, at an undisclosed location, the combined forces of Hughs and Bledsoe "attacked and defeated a party of bushwhackers and tories, numbering some less than 100…killing 17 and taking 2 prisoners and effectually dispersing the whole gang." The Union guerrillas were under the command of "Tinker" Dave

Beatty and Captain Dowdy, but the historical record is largely silent[169] on this combat event. It seemed inevitable that Stokes and Hughs would soon meet on the alluvial plain battlefields flanking the Calfkiller River in White County, Tennessee.

On February 22, Hughs's command—composed of elements of Ferguson's, Carter's and Bledsoe's commands and numbering about sixty—finally encountered a Yankee party "of picked men," totaling 110, led by Captain James T. Exum, Fifth Tennessee cavalry, somewhere south of Sparta and on Calfkiller Creek. The combat, according to Hughs, "was severe in the extreme; men never fought with more desperation or gallantry. Forty-seven of the enemy were killed, 13 wounded and 4 captured; our loss was 2 wounded." It was without a doubt a Confederate victory, yet the prize was marred by behavior not consistent with the rules of war. "Four of my men were killed—3 after they had surrendered," stated Stokes, "and the other after he had been captured." In revenge for the killing of four of Stokes's pickets, Exum refused to treat Hughs's captives as prisoners of war and murdered several straggling Rebels who fell into their hands.[170] This humiliating defeat came to be known to the Fifth Cavalry as the "Calfkiller Massacre." Its memory became a rationale to seek revenge on innocent civilians when pursuing guerrillas and bushwhackers in south-central middle Tennessee for the ruthless Major General Robert H. Milroy. According to one story about the Fifth Cavalry appearing just four months later, they still remembered the "'calfkiller' massacre, and are avenging it terribly."[171]

Colonel Stokes summed up his experience, opinion, leadership abilities and intelligence of his foe Colonel Hughs this way: "I have ascertained that the country is infested with a great number of rebel soldiers under…Col. Hughs, a brave, vigilant, and energetic officer. There is little or no robbing… their attention being directed toward my men. Col. Hughs' command is well armed…Their number at least 600 fighting men."[172]

Hughs may have thought that discretion was the better part of valor when contemplating another tangle with the Fifth Cavalry. In any event, he left his White County camp and again seized the initiative, planning a swift hit-and-run attack on Washington, Tennessee, in Rhea County on February 26.

The raid itself was directed at the Federal courier line and conducted by Champ Ferguson with a force of 150 men. The town's provost marshal was murdered, while all the couriers from Washington to Sulphur Springs were attacked by the guerrillas, wounding two, killing one and taking eleven horses and eleven repeating rifles.[173] Hughs's brief accounting put the number of prisoners at sixty-five, with three killed and seven wounded.[174]

The Washington raid was followed the next day by a skirmish in the Sequatchie Valley. On February 27, the veteran guerrillas made short work of a green company of State Guards. Hughs's command captured twenty-three prisoners and entirely eliminated the nascent military organization.[175]

The encounter of March 10[176] took place on the Calfkiller River, White County. Having gotten wind of Hughs, Stokes dispatched Captains Blackburn and Waters on a search-and-destroy mission. Hughs's report claimed that "after about ten minutes severe fighting, I was forced to retire with a loss of 1 killed and 3 wounded; the enemy's loss was 1 killed and three wounded."[177] Stokes, on the other hand, reported that the force of Hughs's men were in concentrated numbers ten miles from Sparta and, "after a stubborn and desperate resistance of 1 hour...succeeded in dispersing and running them into the mountains." Rebel losses were counted at one killed and four slightly wounded.[178]

Stokes deployed a large force to comb Overton County for any Confederate troops or guerrilla forces on March 12. While the men encountered no significant enemy clusters, upon reaching the William Alexander Officer house, they perpetrated the murders of six stray legitimate Confederate soldiers, none of them under Hughs's command. Colonel Stokes crisply reported, "These men had been murdering and robbing Union citizens."[179]

According to local history, however, the Officer home was suddenly surrounded by some two hundred of Stokes's cavalry. Mr. Officer was entertaining seven unarmed Confederate soldiers, one of whom was his son, John Holford, who, as the Federal cavalry approached, leaped into the loft to hide. The other six were powerless to do anything, and they were too far away from their stacked arms inside the house to attempt resistance. Stokes's men deliberately shot the six Confederate cavalrymen.[180] All were killed in the Officer House except Lieutenant Bob Davis, who, although wounded, was carried outside, stood up against the gatepost and shot to death by an impromptu firing squad.[181]

Stokes's cavalry spent the fifteenth feeding their mounts and with 150 men started in pursuit of Hughs, who had crossed the Caney Fork River the day before with a large proportion of his men. Stokes did not realize that Hughs had crossed the river in search of bigger game to the southwest.

As John E. Clark, writing in *North & South Magazine*, made abundantly clear, the Civil War was a railroad war.[182] While they were important to the Federal supply efforts and tactical troop transfer, they were also vulnerable to attack by enemy forces. A prime example of such warfare is illustrated in

Hughs's attack on the Nashville and Chattanooga Railroad near Tullahoma. An excerpt from Hughs sums up the carnage:

On the 16th of March we tore up the Nashville and Chattanooga Railroad near Tullahoma and captured a train of freight cars heavily laden with supplies for the Federal army at Chattanooga. About 60 Yankee soldiers were captured and about 20 Yankee negroes killed. The train and supplies were burned and the engine destroyed.[183]

Hughs was not challenged by Colonel Stokes, who knew nothing of the Confederate's intentions, and in any event, Tullahoma was out of Stokes's operational boundaries. That does not mean that there was no resistance to Hughs's strike.

Captain George R. Hall of the 123rd New York Volunteer Infantry responded to Hughs's attack on the railroad after being tipped off by a local pro-Union citizen. He learned from the informant that Confederate cavalry, numbering about one hundred, were intent on wrecking a United States Military Rail Road train (the Nashville and Chattanooga), saying that they "were going to throw off the first train of cars from Tullahoma and then blow up the bridge across the Elk River."

Captain Hall took the initiative, commandeering the construction train locomotive and quickly moving it to regimental headquarters. After reporting the crisis, his superior officer "immediately sent Company C to take the place of my company (E) and sent my company in pursuit of the enemy."

Hall left camp, moving forward up the railroad with his company, placing a line of skirmishers on either side of the tracks "a reasonable distance in advance." After having marched one and a half miles, he saw the Tullahoma train coming and watched it run "off the track, and heard the firing on the train."

The method for wrecking trains was for the Rebel commander to send pickets to tear up a section of track while the larger part of his force ensconced themselves in the nearby woods. Ideally, as the first of three trains came thundering along, it was followed by two others "close up." The train was soon derailed, and "the second would run into the first and the third into the second before they could be stopped. The Confederates in the meantime sprang from their cover, firing into the train guard, and capturing a few of them." As Lieutenant Robert Cruikshank, 123rd New York Infantry Regiment, wrote to his wife from his camp on the Elk River on March 24: "On this road that is the way they run the trains—three, one after the other."

In this case, the engineer of the second train was alert to the dilemma and stopped before running into the already derailed train ahead of him, as did the third.[184]

Hall reckoned that the wrecked train was about half a mile away from his skirmishers. The lieutenant decided to file to the right into the woods at the double-quick, intending to flank the Rebels. The raiders, however, got wind of his approach and immediately began to withdraw. Still, Company E was able to come up on their flank and, in a line of battle, fired a volley at the train wreckers, who responded in kind. But the Confederates, making a textbook retreat, formed a line of battle twice, although they "made no stand of any account" and made their getaway. After chasing them about one and a half miles, Hall's command "became so fatigued that farther pursuit would have been ineffectual." He marched his company back to the wreck, finding the cars on fire, but they extinguished the flames. The raiders had succeeded in burning three cars. The locomotive, even though it was thrown from the track, sustained little damage.

Within thirty minutes, the remaining Federal prisoners had returned safely to Company E. They had been robbed of "everything valuable," including their clothing. Two men of the First Michigan Engineers were wounded, as was a civilian, who later died of his injury. One black man was killed and one was wounded, contradicting Colonel Hughs's claim of twenty. "The prisoners report that the rebels were commanded by Lieut.-Col. Hughs, formerly of the Twenty-fifth Tennessee."[185] The Elk River Bridge, given that the camp of the 123rd New York was located there, was not burned as Hughs had intended.

Staying ahead of Federal pursuit parties after wrecking the train, the guerrillas camped on the night of the nineteenth at the foot of a mountain in Warren County, near the town of McMinnville. The morning of March 20 was unusual for Hughs's command, not so much because it offered more combat but because they were "for the first and only time, surprised by the enemy while in camp." He suffered a loss of two men killed and some captured, including some valuable personal papers. The Fifth Tennessee Cavalry, according to its own reports, lost seven killed and suffered the capture of two men.[186]

The skirmish on March 20 was witnessed by Lucy Virginia French, a pro-Confederate living in McMinnville. She wrote in her journal that on the morning of the twentieth, Stokes's men were on their way back to Sparta:

> [T]*hey got down the mt. unseen—and surprised the rebels at breakfast—who took off pell-mell up the opposite mt. Looking at its rugged face and*

rocky brow from here, as it lies nearly opposite to us one wonders how they could scale that height on horseback, but they did. As they came out on top of the mt. they made a little stand—one Yankee was wounded and has since died at McM. The rebels lost some of their saddles, blankets etc. in the melee, and one man. He was a wounded man, had been shot somewhere through the body at the R.R. and it is supposed gave out as he reached the top of the mt. and was shot down after he surrendered. He was shot through the head. Mr. Dugan found him…a youth…about 18 years if age…Will not some mother's heart watch for him who shall come no more, and ache with its lonely watching. The Yankees returned soon from the pursuit—and went on to town [McMinnville]—making a great story of the affair by the time they reached there.[187]*

Realizing his precarious position in middle Tennessee and the tenacity with which Stokes was tracking his command, Hughs knew that he needed to buy time to escape, find some sort of cease-fire agreement and offer to surrender to his foe or be overrun by an exceedingly hostile enemy.

Establishing his headquarters in the pro-Confederate town of Livingston, Tennessee, thirty-one miles from the Federally occupied Sparta, Hughs wrote a letter to Stokes intimating that he was ready to surrender, but there were extenuating circumstances. He wished to consult with Major Bledsoe, whose command "has been under my command." Hughs, unfortunately, had "seen but few of them in the last week." He continued:

Colonel, I must insist on your letting me have ample time to see these men. I will be able to give you satisfaction by Saturday or Sunday, and will be sure to give you a positive answer. I think it would be ungenerous and unfair in me to decide so important a matter as this for these men; for the reason that there are a quantity of officers for the number of men, say five (5) Captains, and the same number of Lieutenants. And, Colonel, I will pledge myself that I will allow none of my men to make any hostile movements until I give you full satisfaction; and, in fact, it is not my intention to do further soldiering in these parts, &c.

He would have surrendered on that very day "but for ill health. I have sore eyes and am quite poorly to-day." He felt justified in warning Stokes that there were a number of men claiming to be part of his command "that do not, and most of them are engaged in robbing and stealing" and that he was not responsible for their conduct. He closed the letter defiantly: "Colonel, very respectfully, your enemy." He added bait in his "P.S.: Colonel I prefer bringing all my command at once; I think that would be best."

Colonel Stokes, in Sparta, replied to Hughs on the first of April. The commander of the Fifth Cavalry was "somewhat surprised…as I understood from your first note that all you wanted was to know whether you and you command would be allowed to take the oath or be paroled." It was unfortunate that Hughs could not surrender his command because of ill health. Consequently, to prepare terms for surrender, Stokes sent three officers, with an escort, to Livingston to hear whatever he might have to put forward. Hughs added this caveat: "Time is precious and forage is scarce; I therefore demand an immediate answer, or all correspondence will cease and hostilities against be resumed."[188]

Hughs's *ruse de guerre* had worked, giving him the trophy he had sought: time. If one White County Cherry Creek community woman's diary entry is any indication, Stokes was made a fool in this skirmish of words. According to Amanda McDowell's April 15 entry:

> *Col. Hughs sent* [word] *into Sparta that he was coming in to take the oath and bring his whole command, but he did it just to fool the Yankees. I say (I think) he acted the fool; the Yankees stayed several days longer than they would have done. Of course they will never put any confidence in what he says again. He thinks he is so smart. It will take hard knocking to knock the conceit out of him.*[189]

Soon after hoodwinking Stokes, Hughs determined to return to his regiment, then at Dalton, Georgia. He started out on April 2, with a diminished force of ninety-five officers and men—all he could prevail upon to go with him. Upon arriving within about 20 miles of Morristown, east Tennessee, he learned that Confederate forces had already left the region. Hughs was forced to backtrack the 120 miles and return to Livingston. Two men were captured, and six of the enemy were killed on the return trek.

Upon his return, their horses being exhausted, they took some time to rest and recoup, seizing the opportunity to decide just what sort of tactical maneuvers they might pursue in their evasion of Stokes. The options were to continue fighting or again attempt to return to the army. The latter alternative was preferred, but this time they would make their effort in smaller groups of twenty to thirty.

They began their journeys on April 18 and, as Hughs wrote, "after much difficulty succeeded in reaching the Army of Tennessee, in Dalton,

Georgia, on the 26th April."[190] Upon arrival, he immediately reported to General Joseph E. Johnston, commanding, for instructions; he ordered him to rejoin his brigade. Some of his Tennessee command arrived in Dalton at the same time, led by Captain Gore of the Eighth Tennessee Cavalry. Others arrived on the twenty-sixth, while, astonishingly, "many refused to come out at all, preferring to remain and take the oath of allegiance to the United States Government."

His report delineated the phenomenal accomplishments of his unavoidable exile behind Federal lines. During his eight-month stint in Tennessee, the number of men under his command varied from eighty-five to three hundred, and not generally recognizing the restraints and obedience of true soldiers "under the circumstances, proper discipline could not be enforced, the men came and went pretty much at will, though all mild means were used to maintain discipline."[191]

Hughs believed that had he been duly sanctioned to organize a proper command from the undisciplined bandits in the plateau, he could have gathered a full regiment of cavalry. Besides the guerrillas, there were citizens who had never been in the service, and a number of Confederate deserters "from the infantry in the country…would willingly have rejoined the service as cavalrymen."[192]

Despite such drawbacks in middle Tennessee and Kentucky, "no time was spent in idleness." Hardly a week passed that the command was not in the saddle, "and not a week passed but more or less fighting took place." More than four hundred of the enemy had been killed, while as many as seven hundred were killed or taken prisoner and paroled. His raids had destroyed more than $500,000 of Federal stores, and more than four thousand stands of arms were captured. His operations required the Federals to move eight thousand troops to guard against his anticipated attacks. Above all, he asserted that "our presence afforded protection to a large section of country against the depredations of the gangs of robbers and bushwhackers, who had become a scourge to the Southern citizens."[193]

The nature of guerrilla warfare meant that his force engaged in requisite rapid marches in extremely hilly and rough terrain, quickly exhausting good horses. His command took great care and considerable expense, especially to keep them mounted. Because of the scarcity of provisions and forage, expenditures were very onerous. When circumstances required, receipts were given, but they could not now be honored because all were lost in the March 20 engagement near McMinnville. Moreover, as the civilians were unwilling to take receipts or Confederate scrip for anything they appropriated, Hughs was obligated to pay all expenses out of his own pocket.[194]

It seems most likely that Hughs did not consider himself a guerrilla but rather a soldier in the Army of Tennessee, forced to utilize guerrilla tactics and guerrilla manpower after he took up the mantle of resisting Federal power in the Cumberland Plateau. Indeed, he regretted that he was not authorized to raise a proper cavalry unit, and as a consequence, the men under his command were less disciplined soldiers but more unruly civilians unfamiliar with anything but hit-and-miss small-scale guerrilla warfare. The extent to which Hughs was able to carry out conventional warfare with terrorist bands led by Oliver Hamilton or Champ Ferguson and others goes a long way toward appreciating his military skill and ability as a legitimate Confederate warrior to take the fight to the enemy, surrounded as he was by hostile forces.

Chapter 5

"OUR BATTERIES PROMPTLY RETURNED THEIR FIRE"

Negley's Raid, May 31–June 9, 1862

The term "raid," when taken in the context of the Civil War in Tennessee, usually brings to mind the name Nathan Bedford Forrest and his forays into Murfreesboro, west Tennessee and Kentucky. Yet the first raid in Tennessee's Civil War history was made one month before Forrest's Murfreesboro attack and was led by Union brigadier general James Negley.

In the spring of 1862, Federal major general O.M. Mitchell was alarmed by reports that Confederate forces were passing from Chattanooga across the Tennessee River to occupy Jasper, Winchester and the mountains bordering on the river and the Nashville and Chattanooga Railroad. This posed a threat to Union advances made since the fall of Corinth. Mitchell then determined to send a force to drive back the Confederate advances, assigning General Negley the task.[195] The raid consisted of two columns, one from Stevenson, Alabama, led by Colonel Joshua W. Sill and the other from Columbia, Tennessee, led by Negley. The military governor of Tennessee, who was anxious to open a front in east Tennessee, likewise approved the raid. Mitchell wrote to Major General Don Carlos Buell, "Our entire force of infantry, cavalry, and artillery will hardly fall short of 6,000 men."[196] There is very little documentation to say just how the raid was planned, but Negley's column moved from Columbia through Shelbyville, then Fayetteville and finally moved on to Winchester and Jasper to a position on the western bank of the Tennessee River opposite Chattanooga.[197] Still's column traveled north with the intent of meeting Negley in Jasper, whereupon both would descend on Chattanooga.

General James S. Negley. *Library of Congress.*

Rapidly moving through Confederate territory, Negley's raiders won laurels among east Tennessee Unionists by picking quarrels with Rebels.[198] Confederates sent reinforcements to Chattanooga and to Powell's Valley in Claiborne County to protect the terminus of the Kentucky Railroad only ten miles from Clinton, Tennessee,[199] fearing that an all-out offensive had begun. Deficient intelligence prompted the Confederate commander, Major General E. Kirby Smith, to wire Joseph E. Brown, Georgia's governor, that "Chattanooga is threatened by so superior a force that its evacuation seems almost inevitable." The Rebel commander in Chattanooga, Colonel Danville Leadbetter, was instructed to retreat in the direction of Knoxville if he could not hold the city.[200] Certainly, the success of Negley's Raid was facilitated by faulty intelligence gathering on the part of E. Kirby Smith.

Moving up from Fayetteville, Tennessee, on June 1, Negley's force first attacked Winchester on June 2, as Federal intelligence had learned that Confederates were determined to hold the town. Guarding Winchester was Colonel J.W. Starnes's Third Tennessee Cavalry. Anticipating Negley's superior force, the Third Cavalry was in the process of evacuating the town when the Yankee force dashed into Winchester, hastening the completion of the Rebel withdrawal. A militant Baptist preacher and notorious ranger,

Captain A.D. Trimble,[201] was captured with four of his band. Prominent Confederates assessed fines to compensate Unionists who had lost property and liberty in the absence of Federal rule.[202]

From Winchester, Negley's column moved on toward Jasper. The second Union column, under Colonel Still, linked up with Negley, and Jasper was occupied on the third. The next day, at Sweeden's Cove in Marion County, Confederate cavalry under Nashville's Colonel John Adams suddenly faced Negley's now augmented force of Yankee raiders.

One June 4, after making a forced march of twenty miles over a jagged, almost impassable mountain road and after capturing the enemy's pickets, Negley's force of 4,500 cavalry succeeded at 3:00 p.m. in completely surprising Adams's command encamped at the foot of the mountain. After a quick, sharp fight, Negley routed the Confederates, scattering them "in the wildest disorder, capturing camp, wagons with supplies, and ammunition." Adams's cavalry fled forty-three miles, "strewing the ground for miles with guns, pistols, and swords" without stopping until reaching Chattanooga. The Rebel getaway was so abrupt that Adams left without his hat, sword or horse. Confederate infantry and artillery were crossing the Tennessee River at Shellmound, heading north, but turned back upon witnessing Adams's routed cavalry. Federal losses were put at 2 killed and 7 wounded and the Confederate loss at 20 killed and 12 captured. Major General E. Kirby Smith reported greater losses of 100 killed and missing. Anticipating disaster, Smith immediately sent eight companies (450 men) to Chattanooga, all the available force he had, with instructions to hold Chattanooga as long as possible."[203]

The next objective of Negley's Raid was Chattanooga.[204] Negley's command made demonstrations in force on Chattanooga on the seventh, opening fire with five batteries on Confederate defensive positions at 5:00 p.m.[205] Meanwhile, E. Kirby Smith telegraphed Colonel Benjamin Allston, commanding the First Cavalry Brigade in Kingston to send "such disposable force as you may be able to spare" from Powell's Valley. Allston was to inform the commanding officer at Kingston to send out scouts in the direction of Winchester "and give timely notice of any movement of the enemy."[206] By the seventh, it was clear that Negley intended to attack Chattanooga, and the Confederate high command in Knoxville informed Brigadier General G.L. Stevenson, in charge of Confederate forces at Cumberland Gap, that all supporting forces were being withdrawn from Powell's Valley to protect Knoxville and Chattanooga. Stevenson, now abandoned by his superiors, would "therefore have to rely upon your own resources in the event of being

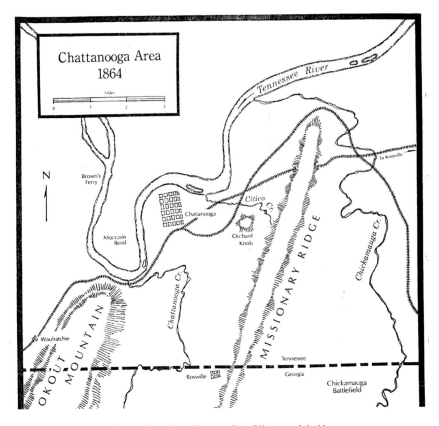

Map of Chattanooga. *Hoobler Collection, Tennessee State Library and Archives.*

attacked."[207] Negley's Raid, although not aimed at such an outcome, caused Confederate forces to be drained from the Cumberland Gap.

Standing on the north bank of the Tennessee River at 8:00 a.m. on June 8, Negley took stock of his situation. He didn't think that Chattanooga would be difficult to take, but because of the lack of pontoon bridge components, rising water, limited supplies and his remote and exposed position, he opted instead for bombarding the Confederate batteries and the city of Chattanooga.[208] Confederate forces on the opposite side of the river were well entrenched close to the river behind earthworks and ready to "dispute our crossing the river at this point." One company of the Seventh Pennsylvania took positions at the river and served as sharpshooters to pick off the enemy's gunners. The remaining cavalry protected the rear. At nine o'clock in the morning, Federal sharpshooters began their work, and Confederate

A twenty-four-pounder cannon. *Library of Congress.*

defenders fired back with a twenty-four-pounder, an eighteen-pounder and four smaller pieces. The Federal field batteries responded in kind with their four-and-a-half-inch Parrott guns. The cannonading was kept up briskly for five hours, after which the Rebel batteries were silenced. Confederates then "beat a hasty retreat" and began to evacuate Chattanooga. Having learned the lessons of "the great panic" after Fort Donelson's fall, Confederate stores were secured and two railroad bridges were burned to encumber an expected Yankee attempt to cross the river.[209]

D.M. Key, a Chattanooga native and attorney, served in the Confederate artillery and left an account of the bombardment in a letter to his wife. According to Key:

A Parrot gun, used in Negley's Raid, early June 1862. *Library of Congress.*

The cannon played on each other from then till dark, the sharpshooters of both Armies in the meantime firing at each other across the river. Night ended the conflict...

They threw shells and balls all through Market Street and over the town and far beyond the Crutchfield House. Our guns remained in perfect silence Gen. Smith having ordered them not to fire.[210]

One anonymous Confederate in the city during the bombardment wrote:

The frightful whizzing of the shell...produced the greatest consternation among the women and children, who were seen running...from the river to the centre of the town in the wildest terror, while the most heart-rendering cries and screams of others in the houses frantically illustrated the horrors of war.[211]

Withdrawing from his position, Negley led his force over the mountains to Shelbyville, where he reported to Military Governor Johnson that his mission "had proved successful" despite the adverse results of skirmishes in the Readyville/Woodbury environs. Part of Still's column, acting as protective flank for Negley, met with stiff resistance from Starnes's cavalry near McMinnville. According to Confederate Lucy Virginia French, writing from McMinnville:

> *On Friday the Yankee cavalry rode into town-took...[they took] two prisoners from Starnes' [cavalry]...They only remained an hour or two in town-passing back again at a rapid pace. About an hour and half later, about 180 of Starnes' cavalry [dashed through town]...On Saturday they came back, bringing back all the Yankees but three who had escaped and seven whom they had killed...On...Sunday the Yankees passed down the road again on foot-being released on parole.*[212]

Regardless, Negley returned with eighty Confederate prisoners, a drove of cattle and a larger quantity of horses. His raid had destroyed Chattanooga's batteries and driven Confederate defenders from their earthworks and the city. Perhaps of most value was that, as Negley reported, "the Union people in East Tennessee are wild with joy. They met us along the road by hundreds."[213] Yet his assertion was far from certain in unanticipated quarters.

While Negley seemed to have met with some success in his daring raid, there were some secret murmurs—in Union circles—that the raid worked to disaffect Unionists in east Tennessee and was riddled with examples of depredations committed against the civilian population. In a confidential note to Colonel James B. Fry, chief of staff for Major General D.C. Buell, Assistant Adjutant General Oliver Greene penned:

> *I wish to call the attention of the general to the outrageous proceedings of the recent expedition to Chattanooga...The line of March is one scene of pillage and robbery. His subordinate officers had aided and encouraged and benefited by the depredations. Negley even "laughed at...the outrages which came under his notice." His troops were little more than thieves and robbers.*[214]

And as for the alleged good he did to bolster the spirits of Union men, Greene claimed that those Unionists in Negley's line of March had "been transformed into secessionists by this expedition." Even worse, all men who declared their

Union sentiments along his line of march "were after his retreat either run out of the country or murdered." The expedition was not a success but rather a "miserable failure." "For God's sake let something is done for [their] relief. When you get a little farther east you will hear enough."[215]

Washington Turner, a Confederate from Jasper, was one of those harshly treated by Negley. In his petition to Jefferson Davis, Washington spelled out how he and a number of his pro-Southern friends were robbed by Negley's soldiers, taken prisoner, given no blankets and finally jailed in Shelbyville in a slaughterhouse. He continued, saying, "General Negley issued an order prohibiting the…citizens of Shelbyville from furnishing us with any article of diet…we were taken to the State Penitentiary and incarcerated with thieves, murderers…I remained near four months, while my little children were robbed of everything."[216]

Notwithstanding Greene's assessment, only four days after Negley's foray ended, back "a little farther east," the *New York Times* was ebullient about Negley's Raid, calling it a "Complete Success." Beleaguered "East Tennesseeans came out in crowds along the march and cheered our troops enthusiastically."[217] Perhaps the real importance of Negley's Raid was its serendipity in that it forced Confederate high command in east Tennessee to withdraw forces in and around the Cumberland Gap and concentrate them nearer Chattanooga and in the Cumberland Plateau to help prepare for the Kentucky offensive in the autumn of 1862. But in so doing, Southern strength at the Cumberland Gap was enfeebled to the point that the Rebel works there were taken with no loss of life on June 18, 1862.[218] It may well be that Negley's Raid also served in some measure as a stimulus and prototype for Nathan Bedford Forrest's raid in middle Tennessee in July 1862.

Chapter 6

MAJOR GENERAL WILLIAM T. SHERMAN AND THE OCCUPATION OF MEMPHIS

If a man disturbs the peace, I will kill or remove him.[219]
                                        —*William Tecumseh Sherman*

Major General William T. Sherman's tenure in Memphis provides an object lesson in the beginnings of U.S. Army policy regarding occupation. The occupation of the Bluff City is a facet of Sherman's Civil War career that has received little attention. His actions were made on the basis of local rather than international law and taken to facilitate the Federal cause by transforming the Bluff City from a hotbed of secession into a Union supply depot and base of operations.

Sherman took command of Federal forces in Memphis seven weeks after the city's fall on June 6, 1862.[220] He quickly discovered that the pro-Confederate elements of Memphis had not yet been pacified and that civil government was unable to maintain the peace. Certainly, a majority of the population was not enamored of the Federal occupation.

Sherman sought the cooperation of the city's municipal authorities to maintain order. In a letter to Mayor John Park on July 27, he addressed the question of restoring civil government. He respected law and order, as well as the notion and practice of democratically elected civilian rule, yet he reminded Park that "necessarily the military for the time being must be superior to the civil authority, but…Civil courts and executive officers should still exist and perform duties, without which…municipal bodies

Major General William T. Sherman. *Library of Congress.*

would soon pass into disrespect." To Sherman, this meant that the city would maintain its police force and collect taxes to secure the quiet of the city.[221]

But the Memphis's constabulary was not adequate to the task, and it was clear that the army had to act. On August 14, he issued General Orders No. 72,[222] establishing "assistant provost-marshals of Memphis." These men had the power to burn or pull down disorderly houses and suppress all rioting "by blows, the bayonet, or firing when necessary." Yet matters did not improve to Sherman's liking. On October 25, 1862, he[223] made the city fathers an offer they could not refuse. It was a system whereby he appointed newer assistant provost marshals, one to each ward and each commanding a regiment of infantry and a squadron of cavalry. The city police force would be placed under the authority of the provost marshal and augmented by one hundred civilian peace officers. These officers were held responsible for any crime on their beat. If suspected of a crime, a police officer would be immediately suspended from duty and tried by a military commission. The city would continue to pay the municipal force and appoint new police officers, subject to the approval of the provost marshal.

Civilians violating military orders would be tried by a military commission. Civil courts continued to try civil matters. Soldiers were free from arrest by the city police.[224] All citizens detected in the commission of any crime would be arrested by either city police or military guard. Vagrants, thieves "or men of bad reputation" would be arrested and put to work "on the trenches, roads, or public streets." More serious was the charge of spying. Sherman was clear about what he considered spying activity in Memphis: "Citizens found lurking about the camps or military lines will be arrested and treated as spies. None will…approach Fort Pickering…and…are cautioned that the sentinels have loaded muskets and are ordered to use them." A midnight-to-dawn curfew was established, and all citizens found "in alleys, by-ways, lots not their own, or unusual places...will be locked up for the night."[225]

Sherman also had to control the press. On July 24,[226] he wrote to the editor of the *Memphis Union Appeal*, Samuel Sawyer, "I should come to an understanding at once with the press as well as the people of Memphis... which means control for the interim for the interest, welfare and glory of the whole Government of the United States.[227]

Outrage was expressed by the *Union Appeal*, demanding city officials take the oath of allegiance.[228] The editor thundered that there must be one ruler of Memphis, not two codes of laws, not two corps of military and civilian police responsible

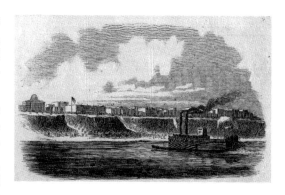

Civil War Memphis and a view of the Bluffs prior to the surrender on June 6, 1862. *From* Harper's Illustrated, *June 23, 1862.*

The Memphis Post Office, June 6, 1862. The Union flag is hoisted over the post office, to the chagrin of the population. *From* Harper's Illustrated, *July 5, 1862.*

to different authorities.[229] Sherman refused to dismiss the city fathers, instead urging the press in Memphis to work for a reestablishment of order. He warned, "If I find the press of Memphis actuated by...a sole devotion to their country I will be their best friend; but if...abusive...then they had better look out, for I regard such as greater enemies...than the men who...have taken muskets and fight us about as hard as we care about."[230]

One reporter who continued to write under a pseudonym was arrested and sent to military prison. This would serve as an example for all reporters who might write articles under "false names." He regarded "all these newspaper harpies as spies" and thought that "they could be punished as such."[231]

By October 11, 1863, Sherman was personally involved in a fight at Collierville, Tennessee. The newspaper account of the story irked him because the author was not identified. He warned the editor, "Don't publish an account…unless the name of the writer is given in full and printed."[232] Newspapers, he said, should "[e]ncourage business advertisements, improvements in the arts, narrations of events abroad in the past or, when well authenticated, of the present. In other words, let the Government and its agents do their business in their own way."[233]

On November 9, 1863, Sherman, on his way to relieve Federal forces in Chattanooga, stopped at Fayetteville (Tennessee) and took time to address letter to J.B. Bingham, editor of the *Memphis Bulletin*. He admitted that he found it hard to define his wishes about press conduct. Freedom of the press, thought and speech were all well and good, but they must have limits because "they generate discord, confusion, and war, resulting in military rule, despotism, and no freedom at all." Proof was found in the previous four decades of American history. "[T]he press has gradually intensified… jealousy and hatred between the North and the South, till war…was bound to result." Sherman closed by telling Bingham, "If a man disturbs the peace, I will kill or remove him…all must act in concert to stop war."[234]

Another unique problem faced by Sherman was that of the swelling contraband population. First, Sherman declared that all contrabands were subject to the laws of the state and city applying to free blacks. He allowed them to work at any trade or calling, to hire out or, if they chose, to return to their former masters, "but no force will be used one way or the other."[235] However, Sherman wanted it known that he was not an abolitionist. It was a matter for the courts, but since the courts had "been destroyed here by our enemy," claims would have to be settled later. Only masters loyal to the Union would be compensated.[236]

The best example of the enforcement of this policy occurred when Sherman was covertly approached by Confederate brigadier general Gideon J. Pillow.[237] Pillow, who seemed to have forgotten that he was a sworn enemy of the United States, wrote about the return of some four hundred slaves missing from one of his plantations. He was certain that they were living in Memphis and threatened "proper reprisals" if they were not returned.[238] Sherman chided the thick-witted Confederate brigadier general that it was "not proper in war thus to communicate or to pass letters." Pillow had no rightful claim.[239]

A fundamental legalistic matter faced by Sherman surfaced when a local judge named Swayne charged a jury to make a finding on all cases involving runaway slaves. The problem was that Judge Swayne utilized old state statutes and charged a grand jury to indict all those who had aided or hired runaway slaves. Sherman wrote to the magistrate saying that old runaway slave laws were contrary to recent Congressional legislation. He urged the judge to stick to prosecuting civil cases and not use a grand jury to test federal law. Sherman would obey the law of Congress, which his army would enforce.[240]

Sherman next faced the matter of capital and confiscation of property. Depositors at the Memphis branch of the Union Bank of Tennessee discovered that the assets of the bank had been, according to Sherman, "removed by force and fraud by Beauregard and others, who have property here which is liable for their unlawful acts." He insisted that the bank officers confiscate those collateral properties and then pay back their depositors. If the bank officers could not "declare boldly and openly against the parties who robbed them," then he had "no alternative but to conclude that they are in complicity with our enemies and treat them as such."[241]

Another concern was currency. A Memphis banker wanted to know which currency would be the most valuable in occupied Memphis—greenbacks, Confederate notes or state notes. "Money," wrote Sherman, "is a thing that cannot be disposed of by an order." It reached its value as a result of trade. It was best to let Union men "feel confident in the determination of our Government" and "despise the street talk of Jews and secessionists."[242]

The cash scarcity in Memphis led the Memphis City Council in November 1862 to propose the issuance of municipal paper money. This violated the U.S. Constitution, and Sherman suggested that the city fathers emulate the example of Mexico, where "the people do their marketing through the medium of cakes of soap." Why not use cotton for money? It had a very convenient price of fifty cents per pound. "Put it up in pounds and fractions and it will form a far better currency than the miserable shinplasters you propose to issue. If cotton is king," suggested Sherman, "it has the genuine stamp and makes money, is money…I suggest that…you set to work and put up cotton in little parcels of 5, 10, 25, and 50 cents."[243]

With the construction of Fort Pickering, Sherman initiated what might well be an early instance of urban displacement and use of eminent domain in Tennessee and American military history. On July 22, 1862, he ordered that all houses inside the area of the planned fort must be vacated. Loyalty was not an issue—military necessity was. A real estate assessment board composed of army officers was empowered to affix a value and issue a certificate stating the worth of the property and the fact that the owner or tenant had been forcibly dispossessed.[244]

Before Sherman assumed command in Memphis, his predecessor, Brigadier General Alvin P. Hovey, issued Special Orders No. 10[245] compelling draft-age Confederates beyond Federal lines. Sherman was presented a protest petition signed by physicians "and others" in Memphis to rescind the order. He refused.

According to Sherman, "it grieves my heart thus to be the instrument of adding to the seeming cruelty and hardship of this unnatural war." Hovey's order would stand. All "who remain in Memphis are supposed to be loyal and true men...all people who are unfriendly should forthwith prepare to depart in such direction as I may hereafter indicate."[246] Since Memphis was a Federal base of operations, the presence of a disloyal population posed unacceptable risks. Such logic escaped Confederate-sympathizers, who imagined that the opposite conclusion was warranted.[247] On July 25, Sherman reported to Grant that he was not satisfied that Rebel sympathies in the Bluff City had been adequately discouraged. "All in Memphis who are hostile to us should be compelled to leave," he wrote. He would deal summarily with any who had aided the Confederate army. Likewise, Grant's orders "that when the head of a family is in the South the family too must go" would be enforced.[248] In an effort to ease shortages of food, Sherman loosened travel restrictions slightly, allowing "free and unobstructed" daytime travel, subject to inspection.[249]

Concerning civilian property rights, Sherman ordered his officers to take "possession of all vacant stores and houses...and have them rented at reasonable rates." The question of rents and property were not involved, only the problem of possession. Therefore, "the rents and profits of houses belonging to our enemies...we hold in trust...according to the future decisions of the proper tribunals...So long as they remain quiet and conform to these laws they are entitled to protection in their property and lives."[250]

Vacant property having been confiscated,[251] the peace was maintained. Notwithstanding these successes, Sherman complained that "still cases are daily referred to me of the most delicate nature," as was epitomized in a confiscation case involving Mrs. Lizzie A. Meriwether.

Mrs. Meriwether was under one government and her husband under another. Her property was improperly confiscated, she said, because it did not matter who ruled Memphis since her husband deeded their property to her. Moreover, Mrs. Meriwether had small children dependent on her. The family's holdings had been confiscated after it had been determined that the property was substantially that of the absent husband.[252] Sherman regarded her argument as an evasion,[253] but in a moment of compassion, he was "willing to stretch the rules as wide as possible to favor distressed women and children." Still, he had forebodings that "a single departure from the rules of severe justice may lead us into many inconsistencies."[254] By early August, dispossessed tenants were provided other houses in Memphis of equal value. Some of the properties appropriated had to be destroyed, while others became hospital facilities. Guards on most major roads into and out of Memphis had been significantly bolstered. New regulations regarding the status of confiscated personal property by the provost guard were set in place. Now any officer or soldier who improperly took any civilian property was "deemed guilty of peculation or pillage and [would be] tried by a general court-martial."[255]

The editor of the *Memphis Bulletin* had printed articles about so-called illegal seizures of property by the Federal army. Sherman responded differentiating between depredations committed by Federal soldiers and excess resulting from "the natural consequence[s] of war." Sherman lectured the editor, "When people…speak contemptuously of the flag…I will not…protect them or their property…war is destruction and nothing else…bear…in mind, that…we are really at war, and much that looks like waste or destruction is only the removal of objects that obstruct our fire, or would afford cover to an enemy."[256]

Sherman enthusiastically endorsed counterinsurgency missions but worried that they would result in guerrilla attacks against ships on the Mississippi River.[257] On September 23, 1862, the steamer *Eugene* was fired on by guerrillas near the town of Randolph.[258] The next day, Sherman ordered the Forty-sixth Ohio Volunteers "to visit the town of Randolph" and "destroy the place, leaving one house to mark the place." This was necessary to let "the people know…we must protect ourselves and the boats which are really carrying stores and merchandise for the benefit of secession families, whose fathers and brothers are in arms against us." On the twenty-sixth, it was reported, "The regiment has returned and Randolph is gone."

The next day, Sherman issued Special Orders No. 254, upping the ante so that entire families were liable for guerrilla attacks on Mississippi River shipping. According to the no-nonsense general, "Whereas many families of known rebels…reside in peace…in Memphis, and whereas the Confederate authorities…sanction…the firing on unarmed boats…it is ordered that for every boat so fired on ten families must be expelled from Memphis."[259]

No one was marked for banishment until a guerrilla attack on the steamships *Gladiator* and *Catahoula* on October 19, 1862. Sherman reported to Grant two days later, "I shall compel ten families to leave for every boat fired on, and let them try whether they prefer to live with their own people or with ours…it is not to be expected that we should feed and clothe the families of men who are engaged in firing upon boats engaged in peaceful commerce."[260]

A few days later, Miss P.A. Fraser of Memphis wrote to Sherman saying that his policy was inhuman. In reply, he suggested that he might lift his sanctions if Confederate authorities would deny that "firing on unarmed boats is...part of the warfare against the Government of the United States." Since Rebel generals had claimed that "Partisan Rangers" were part of the Southern army, they could not disavow these attacks. This being the case, "all their adherents must suffer the penalty." Sherman informed Miss Fraser, "[W]hen the time comes to settle the account we will see which is most cruel—for your partisans to fire... through steamboats with women and children on board...with the curses of hell on their tongues, or for us to say the families of men engaged in such hellish deeds shall not live in peace where the flag of the United States floats."[261] Either it was Confederate policy to fire on unarmed steamboats or it was not. In neither case were such attacks warranted. It was a circumstance that forced people to "appreciate how rapidly Civil War corrupts...the human heart."[262]

Sherman went the extra mile and wrote to Confederate general Theophilus T. Holmes, informing him of his policy and asking if such attacks were part of Confederate strategy.[263] He would wait fifteen days for a reply.

On November 7, 1862, Sherman penned a lengthy reply to a letter from Mrs. Valeria Hurlbut[264] explaining Special Orders No. 254. The fifteen-day grace period was about up, and he had received no answer to his query to General Holmes. Consequently, expulsion was justified because the Confederate "[g]overnment...assumes the full responsibility of the acts of these Partisan Rangers. These men have...fired on steamboats...taking the lives...of peaceful citizens...We regard this as inhuman...and if the Confederate authorities do not disavow them, it amounts to a sanction...of the practice."[265]

The example of Randolph could be but a start. Sherman believed that the "absolute destruction of Memphis, New Orleans, and every city, town and hamlet of the South would not be too severe a punishment to people for attempting to interfere with the navigation of the Mississippi." The major general claimed that he was responding "mildly by requiring the families of men engaged in this barbarous practice to leave and [go] to their own people." As bad as exile was, it was not as bad as "if [Federal forces]...were to fire through the houses of their wives and families." His order was even-tempered by comparison, and he promised that in future cases he would not "be so easy."[266]

Another difficulty Sherman faced in occupied Memphis was that of illegal trade with the enemy, particularly in cotton.[267] In a letter to Grant dated

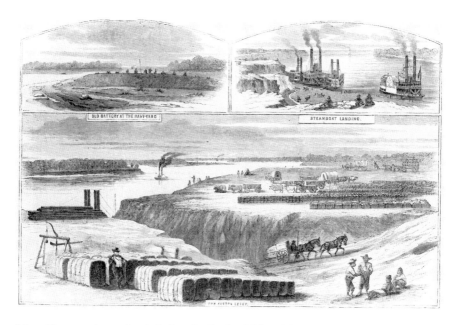

Memphis cotton levee, shortly before the Battle of Memphis. *From* Harper's Illustrated, *March 15, 1862.*

July 30, 1862, he justified his constriction of this commerce and forcible expulsion of Jewish traders from Memphis:

> *I found so many Jews and speculators here trading in cotton, and secessionists had become so open in refusing anything but gold, that I have felt myself bound to stop it. This gold has but one use—the purchase of arms and ammunition...I have respected all permits by yourself or the Secretary of the Treasury, but in these new cases (swarms of Jews) I have stopped it.*[268]

The demand for salt was so great that "many [Jews] succeeded in getting loads of salt out for cotton...Without...gold, silver, and Treasury notes... [the Confederates] cannot get arms...without salt they cannot make bacon and salt beef. We cannot carry on war and trade with a people at the same time."[269] But he was wrong. The need for cotton in Yankee textile mills far exceeded the need to deny the enemy arms and ammunition. In less than a week, Commander in Chief of the U.S. Army major general H.W. Halleck wrote to Grant saying that he had seen "it stated in the newspapers that Gen. Sherman has forbidden the payment of gold for cotton...the Secretary of War...directs me to say...the payment of gold should not be prohibited. Instruct Gen. Sherman accordingly."[270]

Sherman would, of course, obey orders. For the time being, his dispersion of "the flock of Jews" would curtail such trade, but "the whole South… want[s]…arms and provisions…if trade be opened Memphis is better to our enemy than before it was taken."[271]

In late January 1864, a year and a half after his direct involvement in ruling the Bluff City, the command of the District of Memphis, Department of the Tennessee, was given over to Brigadier General R.P. Buckland. Sherman's advice to Buckland provides a good summary of the kinds of things to be wary of when engaged in occupying a city.

He counseled Buckland to look out for any officer whose "style of living [indicates]…he is spending more than his pay, or if you observe him interested in the personal affairs of business men, stop it and send him to some other duty." It was important to keep officers in regimental camps. No new arrival should be allowed to stay in Memphis for more than 24 hours without permission. It was also essential to assure Memphians that if they acted in good faith the government would reciprocate. It was a mistake to have the army serve as the police force. He advised Buckland to "gradually do less and less of it till finally the city and county authorities can take it all off our hands." Fort Pickering should be made impregnable,[272] and the river, levee and "incidentally the town" should be protected. He observed, "I know the poorer classes, the workingmen, are Union, and I would not mind the croaking of the richer classes…power is passing from their hands and they talk of the vulgarity of the new regime…Power and success will soon replace this class of grumblers, and they will gradually disappear as a political power." Buckland should thus encourage "the influx of good laboring men, but give the cold shoulder to the greedy speculators and drones. The moment these…trouble you conscript them…if gamblers, pickpockets, and rowdies come, make a chain gang to clean the streets and work the levee."[273]

During his tenure over Memphis, William Tecumseh Sherman tried to blend civilian with martial rule in order to secure the city as base of operations. He used a heavy hand to be certain, but he could not do otherwise. Securing Memphis meant dealing with a hostile, disloyal, disorderly population and complex issues including property confiscation, expulsion, contraband slaves, the oath of allegiance, civil and martial corruption, judicial and monetary policy and civil government. Since it is implausible that he or any antebellum West Point graduate ever took coursework designed to prepare army officers for the difficulties of occupation, Sherman had no formal model to rely on and, in Memphis at least, broke new ground.[274]

CORRESPONDENCE/GENERAL ORDERS

JUNE 7, 1862.—Skirmish at Readyville, Tenn.
Report of Col. J.W. Starnes, Third Tennessee Cavalry [CSA].
LOUDON, TENN., June 18, 1862.

CAPT.: I have the honor to report that about the 1st of this month I crossed the Cumberland Mountains with 300 men of my regiment, a section of Capt. Kain's battery of artillery, and 80 men under command of Maj. Estes. In accordance with arrangements made with Col.'s Adams and Davis, I moved from Hulbert's Cove to form a junction with them at or near Rutledge's, some 4 miles from Cowen's Depot. On arriving at the point designated I found the enemy passing up the mountain with a force of about 4,500 men, under command of Gen. Negley. Believing I could form a junction with Col.'s Adams and Davis at Jasper before the enemy could reach that point, I recrossed the mountain at night by way of Tracy City. On reaching Tracy City I learned the enemy were already in possession of Jasper, and my command would be entirely cut off from Chattanooga before I could possibly reach there. I determined to shape my course toward McMinnville, by way of Altamont, which I did.

On reaching a point some 6 or 8 miles from McMinnville I learned that a body of the enemy's cavalry were at that place. I immediately moved forward with Capt.'s Thompson's, McLemore's, and D.W. Alexander's companies, overtaking the enemy in Readyville, about 12 miles east of Murfreesborough, capturing 68, killing 8 of their number, and wounding others. I brought the prisoners to the Sparta road, where I thought it expedient to parole them. The party captured was composed of parts of Col. Wynkoop's Pennsylvania regiment, Fourth Kentucky, and about 14 of Andrew Johnson's body guard, under the command of Capt. Ulkhout. The greater portion of the men captured were greatly rejoiced at the idea of being paroled, getting home, and quitting a service with which they were disgusted.

I am gratified to report to the commanding general that during the expedition all the officers and men of my command performed their duty well, and, although arduous, without a murmur.

In making this report I would beg leave to bring to the notice of the commanding general Private Whitset, of Capt. McLemore's company, who acted on one occasion with great gallantry and skill in killing at one shot three of the enemy and a fourth man with the other barrel of his shot-gun.

Respectfully, your obedient servant,

J.W. STARNES, Col., Cmdg. Third Tennessee Cavalry

OXFORD, July 28, 1862.
JEFFERSON DAVIS, President, Richmond, Va.:

The Federals are sweeping this country of its negroes. They have, with bodies of armed men, driven off nearly all the negroes in Arkansas. Phillips County they have neither work stock, corn, nor meat, and rob and plunder the houses. They shoot the negroes attempting to escape, and handcuff and chain those refusing to go. They have driven off all I had—men, women, and children—nearly 400 in number. Can no retaliatory measures be adopted?

G.J. PILLOW, Brig.-Gen.

GENERAL ORDERS, NO. 65., HDQRS. SIXTEENTH ARMY CORPS, Memphis, Tenn., May 26, 1863.

* * * *

VIII. An entire year of occupation of this City by the United States has given abundant opportunity for all persons to make their deliberate election of the sovereignty to which they owe their allegiance. The so-called Confederate Congress by acts passed at an early period of the rebellion ordered peremptorily form the limits of the revolted States those true citizens who adhered to the country of their fathers. The same sentence will be pronounced after one year's patient waiting upon all who while denying their allegiance to the United States yet have found protection beneath its flag. These persons will be sent where their affections are.

IX. Giving aid and comfort to the public enemy is punishable with death and the leniency with which such persons have been treated must cease. Any person who shall hereafter offer insult by word or act to the United States or who shall express sympathy with the enemy or satisfaction at any imagined or real success of the Confederate arms will be arrested at once and severely punished.

* * * *

By order of Maj. Gen. S.A. Hurlbut.

[The following order was more comprehensive, according to a Confederate source.]

Chattanooga Daily Rebel, June 28, 1863

HDQRS. 16th Army Corps
Memphis, May 26, 1863

General Orders, No. 61. All persons residing within the city of Memphis, not in the service of the United States, are hereby required to enroll and register their names with the Provost Marshal, Lieut. Col. M. Smith within twenty days.

II. Such registry must show the character of each person registered under one of these heads:

1.Loyal citizens of the United States;

2. Subjects of foreign, friendly powers

3. Enemies of the United States.

III. Each person who shall enroll him or herself as a loyal citizen shall take and subscribe to the following oath:

United States of America

State of Tennessee

Provost Marshal's Office for the _____ of _____ day of _____1863.

I do solemnly swear, in the presence of Almighty God, that I will bear true allegiance to the United States of America, and will obey and maintain the constitution and laws of the same, and will defend and support the said United States of America against the enemies foreign and domestic, and especially against the rebellious league known as the Confederate States of America.

So help me God.

NOTES

PREFACE

1. Long, *Civil War, Day by Day*, 719.
2. This sum did not include naval actions.
3. Although it was not consulted for this study, see Coffee, Irvine and Matchette, *Military Operations of the Civil War (Guide-Index)*, vol. 4, *Main Western Theater of Operations*, Section M, "Tennessee," 93–153, and Section N, "Tennessee," 178–88. The *Guide-Index* is a very informative work. Section M lists events in an alphabetical format, and Section N lists them in chronological format, both indicating the kind of military action that occurred at the given time and place. There is some brief narration concerning outcomes in Section M but not the duplication of reports, nor does it go beyond the listing of military events. It provides no numerical totals for each kind of event— that is, how many skirmishes, actions, reconaissances, engagements and so on, as are provided herein. Neither appears to provide official records. See "A Preliminary Proposal for a National Heritage Area on the Civil War in Tennessee," Center for Historic Preservation, Middle Tennessee State University, Murfreesboro, Tennessee, March 1995.
4. See *War of the Rebellion: A Compilation of the Official Records of the Union and Confederate Armies* (hereafter *OR*).
5. However, the CD-ROM was incomplete in some cases, so sometimes the paper *OR* and *Official Records of the Union and Confederate Navies* had to be consulted to get a correct citation.

6. See the Tennessee State Library and Archives' (hereafter TSLA) *Tennessee Civil War Sourcebook* online at http://www.tn.gov/tsla/civilwarsourcebook.

7. There is no period or contemporary dictionary of military terms available, according to the U.S. Military Academy Library reference desk at West Point, to give precise definitions for Civil War fights.

8. See *OR*, ser. I, vol. 16, pt. I, 1,020, for example.

9. Ibid., ser. IV, vol. 2, 362.

10. *Nashville Daily Gazette*, November 30, 1861; *Nashville Daily Gazette*, November 30, 1861; *New York Times*, December 8, 1861; *Nashville Daily Gazette*, December 1, 1861; *Trenton (NJ) Standard*, January 10, 1862.

11. Apparently, New York was worth an oath.

12. My thanks to Carole Bucy's "Patient Endurance and Patriotic Devotion" presentation. Bucy is the chairperson of the history department at Volunteer Community College in Gallatin, Tennessee.

13. *Weekly Columbus (GA) Enquirer*, September 30, 1862.

14. *Nashville Daily Union*, February 12, 1864.

15. Works Progress Administration, Civil War Records, vol. 3, 38–39.

16. Loewen, *Lies Across America*, 39.

17. Ibid., 41.

18. And for other states in the Confederacy.

CHAPTER 1

19. *Memphis Daily Appeal*, October 30, November 2–3, 13, 14, 1860, as cited in ProQuest Civil War Records (hereafter PQCW). See also *Semi-Weekly Mississippian*, November 16, 1860, and *Daily Mississippian*, November 27, 1860, as cited in Tennessee State Library and Archives, Nineteenth-Century Newspapers (hereafter TSLA NCN).

20. *Louisville Journal*, December 17, 1860, TSLA NCN; *Milwaukee Daily Sentinel*, December 18, 1860, TSLA NCN.

21. Stevenson, *Thirteen Months*, 31–33.

22. *Memphis Daily Appeal*, April 19, May 2, 1861, PQCW.

23. *OR*, ser. I, vol. 52, pt. II, 67, 154.

24. *Nashville Union and American*, April 24, 1861.

25. 1860 Federal Census Returns, Shelby County, Tennessee, 186, 449–50, 704, 721, 732, 860, 876, 959, 976; 1860 Federal Census Returns, Davidson County, Tennessee, 20, 21, 86, 105, 144, 164, 214, 257, 353, 385, 411, 420, 746. This information was provided by my colleague Steve Rogers.

26. TSLA Broadside Collection; *Nashville Gazette*, April 25, 28, 1861; *Nashville Union and American*, April 25, 1861.

27. *Daily Cleveland Herald*, April 25, 1861, TSLA NCN.

28. Ibid.

29. Wooldridge, *History of Nashville*, 191–92. Although the organization is not referenced in Nashville newspapers after August 1861, it continued its activities. See *Papers of Andrew Johnson*, vol. 5, *1861–1862*, 368, fn 3.

30. *Louisville Journal*, October 28, 1861, as cited from the *New York Times*, October 12, 1861, PQCW. See also *Memphis Daily Appeal*, May 1, 1861.

31. *Milwaukee Daily Sentinel*, March 11, 1861; *Memphis Daily Appeal*, April 14–15, 1861.

32. *Philadelphia Inquirer*, May 16, 1861, TSLA.

33. *Louisville Journal*, May 23, 1861, TSLA NCN; *Bangor Daily Whig Courier*, May 30, 1861, TSLA NCN.

34. *Bangor Daily Whig & Courier*, May 23, 1861, TSLA.

35. Not found during research.

36. *Philadelphia Inquirer*, July 22, 1861, PQCW; *Boston Herald*, August 9, 1861, PQCW.

37. *Louisville Journal*, July 2, 1861.

38. *Louisville Journal*, May 31, 1861, PQCW.

39. *Louisville Journal*, June 4, 1861.

40. *Louisville Journal*, June 3, 1861.

41. *Louisville Journal*, June 5, 1861.

42. Moore, *Rebellion Record*, 2:58.

43. Ibid.

44. McDowell, *Diary of Amanda McDowell*, entry for June 9, 1861.

45. *Louisville Journal*, July 2, 1861.

46. Bolton, *Poor Whites of the Antebellum South*, 165.

47. *Louisville Daily Journal*, June 13, 1861, PQCW.

48. *Harper's Weekly Illustrated* 5, no. 234 (June 22, 1861): 394 (illustration), 397 (text).

49. *The Liberator*, July 19, 1861, TSLA NCN.

50. This is a likely illustration of Bolton's assertion in *Poor Whites in the Antebellum South* that Committees of Vigilance focused on "transient poor white men."

51. That is, a clean shirt—most likely a reference to poor working-class white men being identified because they could not afford a clean shirt.

52. *Frank Leslie's Illustrated Newspaper*, September 14, 1861, TSLA NCN.

53. *Louisville Journal*, August 27, 1861, PQCW.

54. *New York Times*, August 18, 1861.
55. *Louisville Journal*, July 31, August 3, 13, 28, 1861, PQCW; *New York Herald*, August 14, 1862, PQCW; *Nashville Union and American*, July 31, 1861, PQCW, as cited in *Louisville Journal*, August 3, 1861; *New York Herald*, August 14, 1861, PQCW.
56. *OR*, ser. II, vol. 2, 1,369–1,370. See also Frost, *Rebellion in the United States*, 333.
57. *Philadelphia Inquirer*, August 28, 1861; *OR*, ser. I, vol. 52, pt. II, 134–35.
58. *Louisville Daily Journal*, February 26, 1862, PQCW.
59. *Nashville Daily Union*, April 24, 1862, as cited at Vicki Betts, Professional Librarian website.
60. *Memphis Banner*, June 7, 1863.

Chapter 2

61. La Pointe, "Military Hospitals in Memphis," 325–42; Riley and Christie, "Deaths and Disabilities in the Provisional Army of Tennessee," 142–54; *Civil War History* 31, no. 3 (1985).
62. United States Surgeon General's Office, *Medical and Surgical History*, vol. 1, pt. III, 891 (hereafter *Medical and Surgical History*).
63. *Nashville Daily Press*, September 20, 1864; June 6, 1865.
64. Kaser, "Nashville's Women of Pleasure in 1860," 382; *Nashville Daily Press*, September 4, 1863; January 25, 1864; *Nashville Dispatch*, January 24, 28, March 9, August 16, 1864; Memoir of Benton E. Dubbs, Civil War Collection, Box F23, Folder 12, TSLA.
65. *Medical and Surgical History*, 893; Wilson, *Memoirs of the War*, 151–52.
66. *Nashville Dispatch*, July 8, 1863; *Nashville Daily Press*, July 7, 9, 10, 1863; *Medical and Surgical History*, 893; Wilson, *Memoirs of the War*, 152; *Nashville Union*, July 9, 1863.
67. *Nashville Daily Press*, July 9, 15, 1863.
68. *Nashville Daily Press*, July 7, 9, 1863; *Nashville Union*, July 7, 9, 26, 1863; Wilson, *Memoirs of the War*, 152; *Medical and Surgical History*, 893.
69. *Nashville Dispatch*, July 9, 1863; *Nashville Daily Press*, July 9, 1863.
70. *Nashville Daily Press*, July 14, 29, 1863.
71. *Nashville Dispatch*, July 19, 1863; *Nashville Daily Press*, July 20, 1863; *Cincinnati Gazette*, July 16, 1863; *Medical and Surgical History*, 893. See also Wallace, "United States Hospitals," 588.
72. *Medical and Surgical History*, 893; *Nashville Daily Press*, August 6, 12, 1863.

73. *Medical and Surgical History*, 893; *Nashville Daily Press*, August 6, 12, 1863; *Nashville Dispatch*, August 13, 1863; Adams, *Doctors in Blue*, 171.

74. Wallace, "United States Hospitals," 588. See also *Medical and Surgical History*, 894; *Nashville Dispatch*, January 24, 1864; *Nashville Daily Press*, May 4, September 4, 1863; Plaisance and Schelver, "Federal Military Hospitals 166–76.

75. *Medical and Surgical History*, 894; *Nashville Daily Press*, February 15, 1864; Wallace, "United States Hospitals," 588. See also Steiner, *Disease in the Civil War*, 16; Chambers, "Sanitary Report," 3–4.

76. *Medical and Surgical History*, 894.

77. *Nashville Daily Press*, September 10, 1864.

78. *Nashville Daily Press*, December 8, 1864; *Medical and Surgical History*, 894.

79. *Memphis Bulletin*, May 1, 1863.

80. *Memphis Bulletin*, April 30, 1863.

81. TSLA, Federal Collection, Letters, Box F, Folder 24, George Hovey Cadman, 1857–64, Hovey Collection (hereafter George Hovey Cadman Correspondence).

82. *Memphis Daily Bulletin*, August 12, 1863.

83. *Memphis Daily Bulletin*, January 19, April 2, 22, May 7, June 3, 14, 1864; Keating, *History of the City of Memphis*, 1:522–54; *Medical and Surgical History*, 894–95.

84. *Medical and Surgical History*, 895. See also *Memphis Daily Bulletin*, June 7, 1865. In Nashville, the city council attempted to outlaw the practice of some young officers who rode in open carriages with prostitutes. The attempt failed. At one point in Nashville, a young *fille de joie* rode in an open carriage "nude from her waist heavenward," causing quite a disturbance. See *Nashville Daily Press*, May 5–6, August 26, 1863; September 10, 1864.

85. *Memphis Daily Bulletin*, March 8, 1865.

86. *Medical and Surgical History*, 896. See also *Memphis Daily Bulletin*, June 7, 1865.

87. Chambers, "Sanitary Report," 14–15.

CHAPTER 3

88. Studies include Eugene Sloan, "Soule College," *Rutherford County Historical Society* 11 (Summer 1978): 58–103; Robert E. Denney, *Civil War Medicine: Care & Comfort of the Wounded* (New York: Sterling Publishing Company Inc., 1994); John K. Stevens, "Hostages to Hunger: Nutritional Night Blindness in Confederate Armies," *Tennessee*

Historical Quarterly 48, no. 3 (1989): 131–43; Sam L. Clark and H.D. Riley Jr., eds., "Outline and the Organization of the Medical Department of the Confederate Army and Department of Tennessee," *Tennessee Historical Quarterly* 16 (1957): 55–82; Patricia M. La Pointe, "Military Hospitals in Memphis, 1861–1865," *Tennessee Historical Quarterly* 42 no. 4 (1983): 325–42; Harris D. Riley Jr. and Amos Christie, "Deaths and Disabilities in the Provisional Army of Tennessee," *Tennessee Historical Quarterly* 43, no. 2 (1984): 142–54; Glenna Ruth Schroeder-Lein, "Confederate Army of Tennessee Hospitals in Chattanooga," *Journal of East Tennessee History* 66 (1994): 32–58; Urban Grammar Owen, *Letters to Laura: A Confederate Surgeon's Impressions of Four Years of War* (Nashville, TN: Tunstede, 1996); and Ralph C. Gordon, "Hospital Trains of the Army of the Cumberland," *Tennessee Historical Quarterly* 51, no. 3 (1992): 147–56. *Medical and Surgical History* notes nothing of public health initiatives in Tennessee cities, save for an account of the prostitution problem in Memphis.

89. See Jones, "Municipal Vice," pt. I, 33–36.

90. See TSLA's *Tennessee Civil War Sourcebook* online.

91. *Clarksville Chronicle*, February 7, 1862.

92. Spence, *Diary of the Civil War*, entry for March 15, 1863.

93. McGee, *History of the 72d*, 118, diary entry for April 15, 1863.

94. Spence, *Diary of the Civil War*, entry for November 30, 1863.

95. *Fayetteville Observer*, April 23, 1863.

96. *Nashville Daily Press*, May 11, 1863.

97. *Nashville Dispatch*, June 2, 1863.

98. *Nashville Daily Press*, June 11, 1863; *Nashville Dispatch*, June 12, 1863. These actions are not reflected in the Nashville City Board of Aldermen Minutes.

99. *Nashville Dispatch*, July 9, 1863.

100. *Nashville Dispatch*, July 23, 1863.

101. Pierre-Francois Lubin, a nineteenth-century French perfumer. The Paris house of Lubin was founded in 1798 and quickly gained renown in Paris. Lubin scents were worn by Empress Josephine and Princess Borghese, Napoleon Bonaparte's sister. Lubin fragrances made their way to America in 1830. Cited at the Crazy Jay Blue blog.

102. *Nashville Daily Press*, September 4, 1863.

103. Ibid.

104. Ibid.

105. Blood poisoning.

106. *Nashville Daily Press*, September 14, 1863.

107. *New York Times*, August 21, 1863.

108. Presumably, this referred to corruption attendant to army contracts in Murfreesboro made for the improvement of public health.

109. *Nashville Daily Press*, September 14, 1863.

110. *Nashville Dispatch*, November 24, 1863.

111. Ibid.

112. Ibid.

113. A full discussion of the prostitution predicament can be found in Jones, "Tale of Two Cities: The Hidden Battle Against Venereal Disease," 270–76. See also *Memphis Bulletin*, April 30, May 1, 1863; *New York Times*, June 2, 1865.

114. *Nashville Dispatch*, February 6, 1864; November 24, 1864.

115. *Nashville Dispatch*, January 29, 1864. This order is not found in the *OR*.

116. *Nashville Dispatch*, February 6, 1864.

117. Powers, *Hospital Pencillings*, 42.

118. *Nashville Dispatch*, January 28, 1864.

119. Ibid.

120. Ibid.

121. Ibid.

122. Ibid.

123. *Nashville Dispatch*, February 5, 1864.

124. Ibid.

125. *Nashville Dispatch*, March 15, 19, 1864

126. *Nashville Dispatch*, March 24, 1864.

127. *Nashville Dispatch*, March 29, 1864.

128. *Nashville Dispatch*, March 30. 1864.

129. *Nashville Dispatch*, April 14, 1864.

130. Powers, *Hospital Pencillings*, 42–43.

131. *Nashville Dispatch*, April 6, 1864.

132. *Nashville Dispatch*, April 7, 1864. See also *Memphis Bulletin*, March 18, 1864.

133. *Nashville Dispatch*, April 14, 1864.

134. Nashville Board of Aldermen minutes, meetings of March 21, 1862; November 25, 1862; March 10, 1863; April 10, 1863; June 9, 1863; June 23, 1863; September 22, 1863; October 30, 1863; February 9, 1864; March 9, 1864; April 12, 1864.

135. In Roman mythology, Cloacina ("sewer" or "purifier" in archaic Latin) was the goddess who presided over the Cloaca Maxima, the system of

sewers in Rome. Also called Cluacina or Venus Cluacina, her name derives from *cloaca*, the Roman word for sewer.

136. *Nashville Daily Times and True Union*, September 14, 1864.

137. Ikard, "Short and Stormy Nashville Career of Joseph Jones," 209–17.

CHAPTER 4

138. Generally spelled "Hughes" in newspaper reports.

139. *Papers of Andrew Johnson*, vol. 6, fn 2, page 539.

140. *OR*, ser. I, vol. 7, 82, 111.

141. *OR*, ser. I, vol. 16, pt. I, 130–131.

142. *OR*, ser. I, vol. 20, pt. I, 173, 890.

143. *OR*, ser. I, vol. 23, pt. I, 601.

144. Some evidence exists, however, that Hughs was in Kentucky when ordered to "proceed to Middle Tennessee," possibly as early as June or July 1863, when he received his orders from General Bragg. See *Louisville Daily Journal*, July 22, 1863.

145. *OR*, ser. I, pt. II, 646.

146. Hughs does not say what county.

147. Enactment of U.S. Army General Orders No. 100 on April 24, 1863, sharpened the focus on guerrilla warfare and its consequences. *OR*, ser. II, vol. 5, 666–67, 671–82.

148. *OR*, ser. I, pt. II, 646.

149. Word must have spread quickly about Hughs's activities. In the September 8, 1863 issue of the *Louisville Daily Journal*, it was reported that a resident of Jimtown, Kentucky, had been abducted by "a band of guerrillas under the leadership of Col. Hamilton and Capt. Hughes, who are reported to be in the rebel army." See Brents, *Patriots and Guerrillas of East Tennessee and Kentucky*, 65. Beatty was a Union guerrilla leader on the Cumberland Plateau sharing the same notoriety as Champ Ferguson, the Confederate partisan leader. See Moore, *Anecdotes, Poetry and Incidents*, 383. See also Duke, *History of Morgan's Cavalry*, 416–18.

150. *OR*, ser. I, vol. 30, 647.

151. *Louisville Daily Journal*, September 24, 1863.

152. *OR*, ser. I, vol. 30, pt. II, 581–84; *Louisville Daily Journal*, October 9, 1863. Today, Turkey Neck Bend is the site of the Cumberland River Ferry, the only ferry owned and operated by the Commonwealth of Kentucky. It connects two segments of Highway 214 and leads to the scenic Turkey

Neck Bend area of Monroe County. See also *Boston Daily Advertiser*, October 9, 1863; *Daily Dispatch*, October 11, 1863; *Memphis Daily Appeal*, October 31, 1863; *Louisville Daily Journal*, October 30, 1863.

153. *Milwaukee Daily Sentinel*, October 8, 1863; *OR*, ser. I, pt. II, 646–47.

154. *Milwaukee Daily Sentinel*, October 9, 1863; *Louisville Daily Sentinel*, September 10, 15, 1863.

155. *Louisville Daily Journal*, September 25, 1863.

156. A relatively obscure Confederate cavalry commander from east Tennessee apparently caught behind the lines, as was Hughs. See *OR*, ser. I, vols. 18, 31, 32, 38.

157. Ibid., ser. I, vol. 31, pt. I, 574–75.

158. Ibid., 575. The *OR* reveals nothing further about the raid on Monticello.

159. Possibly inflated by Brownlow; it was probably more like fifty.

160. *OR*, ser. I, vol. 31, pt. I, 591.

161. Ibid., 575.

162. Ibid. Aside from Hughs's report, there is little else in the *OR* about the Scottsville Raid.

163. *Louisville Daily Journal*, February 3, 1864. The discrepancy between the December 8, 1863 date that Hughs gives in his official report for his raid on Scottsville and the date given by the *Louisville Daily Journal* is difficult to explain. Perhaps Hughs's records were incorrect or he was reporting from memory, or perhaps it took the three months to the date in his report, December 8, 1863, for news of the event to reach the press in February 3, 1864. The *Daily Journal* story is taken from a "private letter" dated January 30, 1864, about the raid. Its verisimilitude is adequate to cite in this context. It is a conundrum to be certain. Still, both mention Captain Gillum (or Gilliam) and the Fifty-second Kentucky Mounted Infantry). The *New York Herald* of January 31, 1864, printed a story of less detail about the raid.

164. *Louisville Daily Journal*, February 3, 1864.

165. *OR*, ser. I, vol. 31, pt. I, 575. Livingston is the county seat of Overton County. Livingston, being a pro-Confederate town, was not pillaged.

166. Ibid., ser. I, vol. 32, pt. I, 55.

167. Ibid., 8.

168. Ibid., 162–63.

169. Ibid., 55.

170. Ibid., 55, 416.

171. *Chattanooga Daily Gazette*, June 21, 1864. See also Bradley, *With Blood and Fire*. This work is without doubt a compelling and singularly important

book exposing the criminal activities perpetrated by the Federal forces in middle Tennessee.

172. *OR*, ser. I, vol. 32, pt. I, 416.

173. Ibid., 55, 485.

174. Ibid., 55.

175. Ibid.

176. On the eleventh, according to Colonel Stokes in *OR*, ser. I, vol. 32, pt. I, 494.

177. *OR*, ser. I, vol. 32, pt. I, 55.

178. Ibid., 494.

179. Ibid., 495.

180. Only one, contrary to Stokes's report and local record, was a Texas Ranger: William Slaughter. Lieutenant Bob Davis, Oliver Shipp and John P. York were members of the Eighth Texas Cavalry, and William Lipscomb was in the Third Regiment of Alabama Cavalry.

181. The bullet-ridden wooden gatepost is on exhibit at the Overton County Museum, while six headstones mark the graves of the soldiers killed standing at attention and file. The Officer House was listed on the National Register of Historic Places in May 2001. Information was gleaned from the "Officer Farmstead" National Register File on deposit at the Tennessee State Historic Preservation Office, Nashville, Tennessee.

182. Clark, "Railroads and the Civil War," 72–79.

183. *OR*, ser. I, vol. 32, pt. I, 57.

184. Robert Cruikshank Letters, letter of March 24, 1864, as cited at the Town of Salem, New York, website, http://www.salem-ny.com/1863letters. html. See also *Nashville Dispatch*, March 18, 1864.

185. Robert Cruikshank Letters, letter of March 24, 1864.

186. *OR*, ser. I. vol. 32. pt. I, 56.

187. War Journal of Lucy Virginia French, March 20, 1864, TSLA, Manuscripts Division.

188. *Louisville Daily Journal*, April 18, 1864.

189. McDowell, *Diary of Amanda McDowell*, 234–35.

190. Evidence exists to suggest that Hughs may have returned to fight again in a similar capacity in Tennessee about one year after he reported for duty in Georgia. *OR*, ser. I, vol. 32, pt. I, 671, and ser. I, vol. 42, pt. III, 1,203.

191. *OR*, ser. I. vol. 32. pt. I, 56–57.

192. Ibid.

193. Ibid.

194. Ibid.

CHAPTER 5

195. *OR*, ser. I, vol. 10, pt. II, 282–83. Negley was from Pennsylvania and served in the Mexican-American War, as well as had served with Don Carlos Buell in Kentucky as a brigadier of U.S. Volunteers. Before the Battle of Stones River, he worked to reduce the guerrilla menace in middle Tennessee in the Columbia environs. He served brilliantly at Stones River. He was promoted to major general as a result of his commanding. He served later in the Tullahoma Campaign, which pushed Bragg and the Army of Tennessee out of the Volunteer State. His career all but ended at the Battle of Chickamauga as a result of his poor performance while commanding the Second Division of Thomas's XIV Corps. Subsequently cleared of charges of cowardice and desertion, he was never again given a field command. He resigned in January 1865, maintaining that it was the prejudice of West Pointers against civilian officers that led to his fall. He died in New Jersey on August 7, 1901.

196. Ibid., 257, 271–72.

197. Moore, *Rebellion Record*, 5:188–89. In the *Official Atlas to Accompany the Official Records*, plate CXVII (1), indicates that the route taken by Negley was Columbia, Lewisburg, Fayetteville, Salem, Winchester, Jasper, Sweden's Cove (opposite Chattanooga), withdrawal from opposite Chattanooga, Tantalon, Cowan and Normandy, terminating in Shelbyville. Confederate intelligence, however, placed the movement of the raiders from Winchester to McMinnville, then south to Jasper and finally to the gates of Chattanooga. See also *OR*, ser. I, vol. 10, pt. I, 53, 920.

198. *OR*, ser. I, vol. 10, pt. I, 53, 920.

199. *OR*, ser. I, vol. 10, pt. II, 598–99.

200. Ibid., 596.

201. There is no mention of Captain A.D. Trimble in the *OR*. Trimble was the founding minister of the Missionary Baptist Church of Winchester. He possessed $7,000 in real and $8,000 in personal property in 1860. After service with the Eighth Company, Tennessee Provisional Artillery, as well as his capture and release, he returned to Winchester. *Papers of Andrew Johnson*, vol. 5, 435, cited in Rhoton, "Brief History of Franklin County," 76.

202. Moore, *Rebellion Record*, 5:188.

203. *OR*, ser. I, vol. 10, pt. I, 903–5. It may well have been that Adams's command had not been tempered in the furnace of war.

204. His activities were important enough for Smith to keep Robert E. Lee posted. See *OR*, ser. I, vol. 10, pt. II, 596, 903–5.

205. *OR*, ser. I, vol. 10, pt. I, 922.

206. Ibid., 596.

207. Ibid., 598–99, 601.

208. *OR*, ser. I, vol. 10, pt. I, 919.

209. Ibid., 919–22.

210. David M. Key Collection and Scrapbooks, Chattanooga Public Library.

211. Moore, *Rebellion Record*, 5:189–90.

212. War Journal of Lucy Virginia French, June 9, 1862. According to Colonel J.W. Starnes, Third Tennessee Cavalry (CSA), he overtook "the enemy at Readyville, about 12 miles east of Murfreesborough, capturing 68 and killing 8 of their number, and wounding others." The date of his report was June 18, and he does not identify the date of the skirmish, although the *OR* places it at June 7—that is, Starnes could have been mistaken as to the date of the skirmish. Negley was still opposite Chattanooga at the time. Perhaps the Federal troops were a detachment sent on a scout prior to prepare the way for Negley's withdrawal from the shores of the Tennessee River. Starnes's official report can be located in the appendix of this book. See also *OR*, ser. I, vol. 10, pt. I, 917–18.

213. *OR*, ser. I, vol. 10, pt. I, 920; Moore, *Rebellion Record*, 5:188.

214. *OR*, ser. I, vol. 16, pt. II, 40.

215. Ibid.

216. *OR*, ser. II, vol. 5, 805. Most likely, Mr. Washington never received remuneration from Jefferson Davis or Military Governor Andrew Johnson.

217. *New York Times*, June 13, 1862.

218. Federal forces had evacuated the Cumberland Gap by October 3, 1862, after a long siege by Confederate forces and just five days before the Battle of Perryville, Kentucky. Thus, the Gap was held by Union forces during Bragg's invasion of Kentucky, making his offensive perhaps longer and more arduous than it might have otherwise been. Perhaps the fact that Union forces held the Gap resulted in logistical problems for Bragg, thus contributing to his defeat in Kentucky. In any event, it was clear for the Confederate retreat. See *OR*, ser. I, vol. 16, pt. I, 990; vol. 52, pt. I, 49–51.

Chapter 6

219. *OR*, ser. I, vol. 31, pt. III, 97–98.

220. *OR*, ser. I, vol. 17, pt. II, 110–11, General Orders No. 56.

221. Ibid., 127.

222. The *Memphis Union Appeal* of August 27, 1862, printed the same order, but it was erroneously identified as "SPECIAL ORDER No. 180."

223. *OR*, ser. I, vol. 17, pt. II, 294–96.

224. Except when caught in the act of committing a crime by a city constable.

225. *OR*, ser. I, vol. 17, pt. II, 294–96.

226. Ibid., 116–17.

227. Ibid.

228. There was no officially sanctioned oath, but the version then used in New Orleans was most likely used in Memphis: "I solemnly swear that I will bear true allegiance to the Government of the United States of America, that I will support and obey the constitution and laws thereof—and I hereby renounce all fealty and allegiance to the so-called 'Confederate States of America.'" See the *Memphis Union and Appeal*, July 1, 1862.

229. *Memphis Union Appeal*, July 23, 1862.

230. *OR*, ser. I, vol. 17, pt. II, 116–17.

231. Ibid., 178–79.

232. *OR*, ser. I, vol. 31, pt. I, 766.

233. Ibid., 848.

234. *OR*, ser. I, vol. 31, pt. III, 97–98.

235. *OR*, ser. I, vol. 17, pt. II, 294–96.

236. Ibid., 158–60.

237. Pillow had earlier made an appeal to President Jefferson C. Davis. He must have thought that his luck would be better by getting in touch with Major General Sherman. *OR*, ser. I, vol. 52, pt. II, 32. See the appendix of this book for Pillow's appeal.

238. *OR*, ser. I, vol. 17, pt. II, 169–70.

239. Ibid., 170–72. Pillow would in November 1864 make another attempt to gain Sherman's permission to cross enemy lines to protect his plantation property in Maury County, Clifton. The request was approved, conditional to Pillow's taking the oath. See *OR*, ser. I, vol. 39, pt. III, 640–41.

240. *OR*, ser. I, vol. 17, pt. II, 863–65. It was apparently an offer that Swayne could not refuse. Sherman later spoke to the President Washington Union Club in Memphis, reiterating many of the same notions. See *OR*, ser. I, vol. 17, pt. II, 869–70. See also *OR*, ser. I, vol. 17, pt. II, 865–66.

241. *OR*, ser. I, vol. 17, pt. II, 161–62. See also *Papers of Andrew Johnson*, vol. 5, 606–7.

242. *OR*, ser. I, vol. 17, pt. II, 868.

243. Ibid., 875.

244. Ibid., 112–13.

245. Not found. This was apparently Special Orders No. 14, issued on July 10, 1862. The *OR* does not reference this order directly, although correspondence from Brigadier General M. Jeff. Thompson on Special Service, CSA, to Major General U.S. Grant on July 14, does reference the order. According to Confederate brigadier general Thompson, he had read a "copy of your Special Orders, No. 14, of July 10, ordering the families of certain parties therein named to leave your lines within five days." In essence, those who would not take the oath of allegiance to the United States would be expelled from Memphis. Thompson lectured the Federal commander that he "must not for a moment suppose that the thousands who will be utterly unable to leave and the many who will thus be forced to take the hateful oath of allegiance to a despised government are to be thus converted into loyal citizens of the United States or weaned from their affections for our glorious young confederacy; and whole to 'threaten' were unsoldierly, yet to 'warn' is kindness, and therefore, general, I would tell you to beware of the curses and oaths of vengeance which the 50,000 brave Tennessee who are still in our army will register in heaven against the persecutor of helpless old men, women, and children, and the general who cannot guard his own lines." Neither Grant nor Sherman was impressed with the sermon. *OR*, ser. I, vol. 17, pt. II, 98–99. See also *OR*, ser. I, vol. 17, pt. II, 121–23.

246. *OR*, ser. I, vol. 17, pt. II, 114.

247. Federal generals were not the only ones making such edicts. For example, Confederate general E. Kirby Smith in Knoxville issued one on April 23, 1861. See *OR*, ser. I, vol. 10, pt. II, 640–64; *OR*, ser. II, vol. 1, 882, 884.

248. *OR*, ser. I, vol. 17, pt. II, 122.

249. Ibid., 117–18.

250. Ibid., 156–57.

251. Ibid., 156.

252. Ibid., 169–71.

253. Ibid., 156–57.

254. Ibid., 169–71.

255. Ibid., 200–202, 204, 219–20.

256. Sherman, *Memoirs of General W.T. Sherman*, 298–301. Sherman's reply is found only in these memoirs.

257. *OR*, ser. I, vol. 17, pt. II, 201–2.

258. In Tipton County.

259. *OR*, ser. I, vol. 17, pt. II, 240.

260. Ibid., 285–86. There seems to be no information available regarding any expulsion resulting from this order. General Orders No. 65,

however, was explicit. *OR*, ser. II, vol. 5, 711. See the appendix of this book for the order.

261. *OR*, ser. I, vol. 17, pt. II, 288.

262. Ibid. Sherman also hoped that Confederate women in Memphis would realize their role in preventing guerrilla attacks. "Would to God ladies better acted their mission on earth; that instead of inflaming the minds of their husbands and brothers to lift their hands against the Government of their birth and stain them in blood, had prayed them to forbear, to exhaust all the remedies afforded them by our glorious Constitution, and thereby avoid 'horrid war,' the last remedy on earth."

263. *OR*, ser. I, vol. 17, pt. II, 288. (Sherman signed the letter "Your friend.")

264. Apparently no relation to Federal major general S.A. Hurlbut.

265. *OR*, ser. I, vol. 17, pt. II, 860.

266. Ibid.

267. *Memphis Union Appeal*, July 10, 1862; *OR*, ser. I, vol. 17, pt. II, 120, 123.

268. *OR*, ser. I, vol. 17, pt. II, 140–41.

269. Ibid.

270. Ibid., 150.

271. *OR*, ser. III, vol. 2, 349. See also *OR*, ser. I, vol. 17, pt. II, 178–79; *OR*, ser. III, vol. 2, 382; *OR*, ser. I, vol., 17, 189; *OR*, ser. I, vol. 17, pt. II, 171; *OR*, ser. I, vol. 17, pt. II, 187–88.

272. See *OR*, ser. I, vol. 17, pt. II, 351–52.

273. *OR*, ser. I, vol. 32, pt. II, 238–39.

274. Ibid. Sherman's superior, Major General U.S. Grant, carried out similar occupation policies in Paducah, Kentucky, in 1861, complete with offensive references to Jews. It can be thus argued that Sherman's efforts were largely derivative. Moreover, before the Civil War, General Winfield Scott carried out what some historians have anecdotally called "a model" or "textbook" example occupation of Mexico City. Grant was in Mexico at the time, serving as a regimental supply officer, and so he may have learned "how to occupy" a city from his experience there. One question that remains is whether or not the actions of Scott, Grant, Sherman, Butler and other Federal as well as Confederate generals in this regard helped form the basis for future occupation policy in impending wars in which America would become involved. If they provided "textbook" examples, in what textbooks are they found? Research into the evolution of occupation policies pursued in the Mexican-American War, the Spanish-American War and Filipino Insurrection, as well as up through the war in Vietnam and the Gulf War, could prove an avenue of useful research. In

a more immediate sense, a comparison of Sherman's policies with those carried out by Confederate major general E. Kirby Smith in Knoxville may prove an excellent place to start, at least insofar as Tennessee Civil War history is concerned. See also Nicholas, *Martial Law*.

BIBLIOGRAPHY

A large and comprehensive source for all things related to the Civil War in Tennessee can be found online at http://www.tn.gov/tsla/ civilwarsourcebook. This is the extended bibliography for the Tennessee State Library and Archives (TSLA) *Tennessee Civil War Sourcebook*.

PUBLICATIONS

Adams, George W. *Doctors in Blue: The Medical History of the Union Army in the Civil War*. New York: H. Schumen,1952.

Bolton, Charles C. *Poor Whites of the Antebellum South: Tenants and Laborers in Central North Carolina and Northeast Mississippi*. Durham, NC: Duke University Press, 2003.

Bradley, Michael R. *With Blood and Fire: Life Behind Union Lines in Middle Tennessee, 1863-65*. Shippensburg, PA: Burd Street Press, 2003.

Brents, John A., Major. *The Patriots and Guerrillas of East Tennessee and Kentucky; The Sufferings of the Patriots. Also the Experience of the Author as an Officer in the Union Army. Including Sketches of Noted Guerrillas and Distinguished Patriots*. N.p.: self-published, 1868.

Broadfoot, Thomas, comp. *The War of the Rebellion: a Compilation of the Official Records of the Union and Confederate Armies*. 128 vols. Series I–IV, 1890–1901. CD-ROM, 2000. Washington, D.C.: United States War Department.

Center for Historic Preservation, Middle Tennessee State University. "A Preliminary Proposal for a National Heritage Area on the Civil War in Tennessee." Murfreesboro, Tennessee, March 1995.

Chambers, William M. "Sanitary Report of the Condition of the Prostitutes of Nashville," January 31, 1865. William P. Palmer Collection, Western Reserve Historical Society, Cleveland, Ohio.

Clark, John E. "Railroads and the Civil War. "*North & South* 10, no. 5 (March 2008).

Clark, Sam L., and H.D. Riley Jr., eds. "Outline and the Organization of the Medical Department of the Confederate Army and Department of Tennessee." *Tennessee Historical Quarterly* 16 (1957).

Coffee, Edwin R., Dallas Irvine and Robert Matchette, comps. *Military Operations of the Civil War: A Guide-Index to the Official Records of the Union and Confederate Armies, 1861–1865*. Vol. 4, *Main Western Theater of Operations, Except Gulf Approach, 1861–1863* ['65?]. Section M, "Tennessee," and Section N, "Tennessee." Washington, D.C.: NARA, General Services Administration, 1980.

Denney, Robert E. *Civil War Medicine: Care & Comfort of the Wounded*. New York: Sterling Publishing Company Inc., 1994.

Duke, Basil W. *History of Morgan's Cavalry*. Cincinnati, OH: Miami Printing and Publishing Company, 1867.

Frost, Janette Blakeslee. *The Rebellion in the United States, or, The War of 1861: Being a Complete History of Its Rise and Progress, Commencing with Its Rise and Progress, Commencing with the Presidential Election…*. 2 vols. Boston: Degen, Esgtes and Priest, 1862.

Gordon, Ralph C. "Hospital Trains of the Army of the Cumberland." *Tennessee Historical Quarterly* 51, no. 3 (1992).

Ikard, Robert W. "The Short and Stormy Nashville Career of Joseph Jones, Tennessee's First Public Health Officer." *Tennessee Historical Quarterly* 48 (1989).

Jones, James B., Jr. "The Civil War in Tennessee: New Perspectives on Familiar Materials." *Tennessee Historical Quarterly* 61, no. 2 (Summer 2003).

———. "The Civil War in the Upper Cumberland Region." *Rural Life and Culture in the Upper Cumberland.* Edited by Michael E. Birdwell and Calvin Dickinson. Lexington: University of Kentucky Press, 2004.

———. "'The Moon Must Hold His Nose as He Passes Over This Vast Sea of Filth': The Struggle for Public Health in Civil War Tennessee Cities." *West Tennessee Historical Society Papers* 59 (2007).

———. "Municipal Vice: The Management of Prostitution in Tennessee's Urban Experience. Part I, the Experience of Nashville and Memphis, 1854–1917." *Tennessee Historical Quarterly* 50, no. 1 (Spring 1991).

———. "Negley's Raid." *North & South* 11, no. 2 (December 2008).

———. "The Reign of Terror of the Safety Committee Has Passed Away Forever." A history of Committees of Safety and Vigilance in west and middle Tennessee, 1860–62. *West Tennessee Historical Society Papers* 61 (2009).

———. "A Tale of Two Cities." *North & South* 10, no. 5 (March 2008).

———. "A Tale of Two Cities: The Hidden Battle Against Venereal Disease in Civil War Nashville and Memphis." *Civil War History* 31 (September 1985).

———. "Tennessee Taliban." *North & South* 12, no. 2 (April 2010).

———. "The Tennessee Taliban: A History of Committees of Safety in Nashville and Memphis, 1860–1862." Tennessee Conference of Historians, Cumberland University, Lebanon, Tennessee, September 25–26, 2009.

Kaser, David. "Nashville's Women of Pleasure in 1860." *Tennessee Historical Quarterly* 23, no. 4 (1964).

Keating, John M. *History of the City of Memphis.* 2 vols. Syracuse, NY: O.F. Vedder 1888.

La Pointe, Patricia M. "Military Hospitals in Memphis, 1861–1865." *Tennessee Historical Quarterly* 42, no. 4 (1983).

Loewen, James W. *Lies Across America.* New York: New Press, 1999.

Long, E.B., ed. *The Civil War, Day by Day: An Almanac 1861–1865.* New York: Doubleday, 1971.

Lowry, Thomas P. *The Story the Soldiers Wouldn't Tell: Sex in the Civil War.* Mechanicsburg, PA: Stackpole Books, 1994.

McDowell, Amanda. *Fiddles in the Cumerlands (Diary of Amanda McDowell).* Edited by Lela McDowell Blankenship. New York: Richard R. Smith, 1943.

McGee, B.F. *History of the 72d Indiana Volunteeer Infantry of the Mounted Lightning Brigade…Especially Devoted to Giving the Reader a Definite Knowledge of the Service of the Common Soldier with an Appendix Containing a Complete Roster of Officers and Men.* Lafayette, IN: S. Vetter and Company, 1882.

Memoir of Benton E. Dubbs. Tennessee State Library and Archives. Civil War Collection, Box F23, Folder 12. Nashville, Tennessee.

Moore, Frank, ed. *Anecdotes, Poetry and Incidents of the War: North and South, 1860–1865.* New York: Bible House, 1867.

———. *The Rebellion Record: A Diary of American Events, with Documents, Narratives, Illustrative Events, Poetry.* 11 vols. New York: D. Van Nostrand, Publisher, 1867–68.

Official Atlas to Accompany the Official Records of the War of the Rebellion. Washington, D.C.: Government Printing Office, 1891–95.

Owen, Urban Grammar. *Letters to Laura: A Confederate Surgeon's Impressions of Four Years of War.* Nashville, TN: Tunstede, 1996.

The Papers of Andrew Johnson. Vol. 5, *1861–1862.* Knoxville: University of Tennessee Press, 1979.

Plaisance, Aloysius F., and Leo Schelver III. "Federal Military Hospitals in Nashville, May and June, 1864." *Tennessee Historical Quarterly* 29, no. 2 (1970).

Powers, Elvira J. *Hospital Pencillings; Being a Diary While in Jefferson General Hospital, Jeffersonville, Ind., and Others at Nashville, Tennessee, as Matron and Visitor.* Boston: Edward L. Mitchel, 1866.

Rhoton, Thomas F. "A Brief History of Franklin County." MA thesis, University of Tennessee, 1941.

Riley, Harris D., Jr., and Amos Christie. "Deaths and Disabilities in the Provisional Army of Tennessee." *Tennessee Historical Quarterly* 43, no. 2 (1984).

Schroeder-Lein, Glenna Ruth. "Confederate Army of Tennessee Hospitals in Chattanooga." *Journal of East Tennessee History* 66 (1994).

Sherman, William Tecumseh. *Memoirs of General W.T. Sherman.* New York: Library Classics of the United States, 1990.

Sloan, Eugene. "Soule College." *Rutherford County Historical Society* 11 (Summer 1978).

Spence, John C. *A Diary of the Civil War.* Murfreesboro, TN: Rutherford County Historical Society, 1993.

Steiner, Paul E. *Disease in the Civil War; Natural Biological Warfare in 1861–65.* Springfield, IL: C.C. Thomas, 1968.

Stevenson, William G. *Thirteen Months in the Rebel Army.* New York: A.S. Barnes and Company, 1862.

Tennessee State Historic Preservation Office. "Officer Farmstead." National Register File on deposit. Nashville, Tennessee.

United States Naval War Records Office. *Official Records of the Union and Confederate Navies.* 27 vols. Series I–II. Washington, D.C.: Government Printing Office, 1894–1922.

United States Surgeon General's Office. *The Medical and Surgical History of the War of the Rebellion.* Edited by Charles Smart. Washington, D.C.: Government Printing Office, 1888.

Wallace, R. "United States Hospitals at Nashville." *Cincinnati Lancet and Observer* 7 (October 1864.)

Wilson, Ephraim A. *Memoirs of the War in One Volume.* Cleveland, OH: W.M. Bayne Printing Company, 1893.

Wooldridge, John. *History of Nashville, Tennessee.* Nashville, TN: Goodspeed Publishing, 1886.

PRESENTATIONS

Bucy, Carole. "Patient Endurance and Patriotic Devotion: Experience and Memory of Nashville Women on the Home Front." Presented at the Thirty-third Annual Meeting of the Tennessee Conference of Historians, Tennessee Technical University, September 22, 2000.

Jones, James B., Jr. "Affair at Travisville: Murder, Barbecue, Historical Markers and Public History on the Tennessee Cumberland Plateau." Thirty-second Tennessee Conference of Historians, Volunteer State Community College, Gallatin, Tennessee, September 24–25, 1999.

———. "The Struggle for Public Health in Civil War Memphis." Fifty-third Annual Kentucky-Tennessee American Studies Association, Fall Creek Falls State Park, Pikeville, Tennessee, April 3–5, 2008.

———. "A Tale of Two Cities." Nineteenth Tennessee Conference of Historians, Vanderbilt University, Nashville, Tennessee, April 1986.

———. "William Tecumseh Sherman and the Occupation of Memphis." Fifteenth Annual Ohio Valley History Conference, Tennessee Technological University, Cookeville, Tennessee, October 21–23, 1999.

Websites

Crazy Jay Blue. http://cjblue.blogspot.com/2006_01_01_cjblue_archive. html.

InfoTrac. Tennessee State Library and Archives. http://infotrac.galegroup. com/itw/infomark/110/1/1/purl=rc6_NCNP?sw_aep=nash71688.

Motlow State Community College/Civil War Research Center. http:// cwrc.org/index.html.

Nicholas, S.S. *Martial Law: Part of a Pamphlet First Published in 1842 Over the Signature of a Kentuckian*. Philadelphia, PA: J. Campbell, 1862. Available at http://catalog.hathitrust.org/Record/000588212.

ProQuest Civil War Records. "Civil War Era Newspapers." http://www. proquest.com/en-US/catalogs/databases/detail/cwe.shtml.

Research Your Civil War Ancestor. http://www.researchonline.net.

Son of the South. *Harper's Weekly Illustrated*, 1861–65. http://www. sonofthesouth.net/leefoundation/the-civil-war.htm.

Tennessee Civil War National Heritage Area. http://histpres.mtsu.edu/ tncivwar.

Town of Salem, New York. Robert Cruikshank Letters. http://www.salem-ny.com/1863letters.html.

University of North Carolina Chapel Hill Libraries. Documenting the American South. Academic Affairs Library, electronic editions. http:// docsouth.unc.edu.

Vicki Betts, Professional Librarian, Cataloging and Reference. "Newspaper Introduction." University of Texas–Tyler. http://www. uttyler.edu/vbetts/newspaper_intro.htm. An excellent source with a wide variety of newspaper reports on many aspects of the Civil War in many Confederate states.

METROPOLITAN NASHVILLE/
DAVIDSON COUNTY ARCHIVES

Nashville Board of Aldermen minutes.
Nashville Daily Gazette.
Nashville Daily Press and Times.
Nashville Daily Union.

SPECIAL COLLECTIONS

Corbit Special Collections/University Archives. University of Tennessee–
Martin.

David M. Key Collection and Scrapbooks. Local History Section,
Chattanooga Public Library.

Frank M. Gurnsey Collection. Special Collections of the Mississippi Valley
Collection, University of Memphis.

Hovey Collection. Civil War Collection, Federal Collection, Letters, Box F,
Folder 24. George Hovey Cadman, 1857–64. Tennessee State Library
and Archives.

John Watkins Collection. University of Tennessee Library Special Collections
Division, University of Tennessee–Knoxville.

Wilder Collection. University of Tennessee–Chattanooga, Special
Collections.

Works Progress Administration, Civil War Records. 5 vols. Tennessee State
Library and Archives.

TENNESSEE STATE LIBRARY AND ARCHIVES

Tennessee State Library and Archives Broadside Collection.

War Journal of Lucy Virginia French. On deposit at TSLA, Manuscripts Division.

Microfilm

Civil War Collection, 1861–65, Mfm. 824.

Davidson County, Tennessee, Federal Census Returns for 1860.

Shelby County, Tennessee, Federal Census Returns for 1860.

Manuscripts

Civil War Collection, Confederate and Federal, RG 23.
    Andrew Jackson Lacy, 1862–63. Confederate Collection, Box C 28, Folder 17, Letters.
    Confederate Collection, Box 8, Folder 23.
    Confederate Collection, Mfm 824-3, accession no. 1576, Box 11, Folder 11.
    Ed. R. Harris and wife, letters. Regarding death of Captain John Harris. Confederate Collection, Mfm 824-3, accession no. 1379, Box 9, Folder 22.

Lucy Virginia Smith French Diaries, accession nos. 89-200, 73-25.

Records of the Southern Claims Commission, RG 21.

WESTERN RESERVE HISTORICAL SOCIETY, CLEVELAND, OHIO

William P. Palmer Collection.

PERIOD NEWSPAPERS ON MICROFILM LOCATED AT TSLA

Chattanooga Daily Gazette.
Chattanooga Daily Rebel.
Clarksville Chronicle.
[Humboldt] *Soldier's Budget.*
Knoxville Daily Bulletin.
Knoxville Daily Register.
Knoxville Daily Southern Chronicle.
[Knoxville] *Holston Journal.*
Knoxville Tri-Weekly Whig and Rebel Ventilator.
Memphis Daily Appeal.
Memphis Daily Bulletin.
Memphis Union Appeal.
Memphis Weekly Appeal.
Murfreesboro Daily Rebel Banner.
Nashville Daily Patriot.
Nashville Daily Press and Times.
Nashville Daily Times and True Union.
Nashville Daily Union.
Nashville Union and American.
Trenton Standard.

MIDDLE TENNESSEE STATE UNIVERSITY MICROFILM COLLECTION

New York Times.

About the Author

J ames B. Jones Jr. is a public historian on the staff of the Tennessee Historical Commission/State Historic Preservation Office in Nashville. He has published many books and articles on many topics about Tennessee history, including but not limited to the Civil War. He serves also as the editor of the THC newsletter, the *Courier*. He earned a doctor of arts degree in history and historic preservation from Middle Tennessee State University in 1983. He resides with his spouse in Murfreesboro.

Visit us at
www.historypress.net
....
This title is also available as an e-book